The GLASS HOUSE

THE UNITED NATIONS IN ACTION

The
GLASS HOUSE

The United Nations in Action

James J. Wadsworth

FREDERICK A. PRAEGER, *Publishers*

New York · Washington · London

FREDERICK A. PRAEGER, PUBLISHERS
111 Fourth Avenue, New York, N.Y. 10003, U.S.A.
77–79 Charlotte Street, London, W.1, England

Published in the United States of America in 1966
by Frederick A. Praeger, Inc., Publishers

Printed in the United States of America

To

THE HONORABLE HENRY CABOT LODGE

Mentor, Colleague, Boss, and Friend

Acknowledgments

Heartfelt thanks are due to so many who helped by furnishing information and practical suggestions that I hardly know where to start and how to stop:

To the State Department, through its Bureau of International Organization affairs, and especially Joseph J. Sisco and Richard N. Gardner;

To the United States Mission to the United Nations, and especially Miss Rita Brown, Miss Anne Palmas, and Albert Bender; and

To the United Nations Secretariat, and especially Philippe de Seynes and Jean-Paul Martin.

Introduction

THE GLASS HOUSE is a paradox. There has never before been an international organization that has operated so completely in the glare of world-wide publicity. It is virtually a goldfish bowl, and it is from this, as well as from its physical structure, that the title of this volume is derived. Yet, despite all its translucence and all its brilliant lighting, the United Nations is still widely misunderstood. This is its paradox.

I can well appreciate the confusion created in the minds of people all over the world as they listen to the one voice that speaks for the many voices of this great edifice. After spending eight years in the United Nations representing the United States in various capacities, I certainly cannot claim complete knowledge and understanding of the many shapes it assumes. The United Nations wears many coats, each of many colors; and the coloring often depends entirely upon the national or regional eye that observes it.

My own activities in and around the Glass House may perhaps serve to establish me as a limited expert. The qualifying adjective "limited" is not chosen lightly, nor through mock modesty. It is used because I remember a very wise remark His Holiness Pope Pius XII made to me during a brief audience in 1949, when I was on a mission for the Economic Cooperation Administration. He asked how long my visit to

Rome would be, and upon hearing that, regrettably, it would last less than three days, he exclaimed: "Ah! Then you will return to Washington an 'expert' on Rome and Italy! It is only when one stays for several weeks that one realizes how much there is to learn. And if you should stay for years, you would realize that you would need many more years before becoming a real expert."

So it is with the Glass House. Few Americans have had more varied experience with it than I, and yet I have found that in preparing material for this book, I have been forced to call for help over and over again. My thanks to those who cheerfully answered the call are rendered in the Acknowledgments, but even with all the help I have received, I can still by no means claim to be a complete expert.

The variety of my jobs in the United Nations has been great, which in itself made my experience fascinating. I was sworn in on February 23, 1953, as Deputy U.S. Representative to the United Nations and to the Security Council. With the selfless nonpartisan help of Ambassador Ernest A. Gross, my predecessor, Ambassador Henry Cabot Lodge, the U.S. Representative, and I then prepared for the resumed session of the Seventh General Assembly. But before that session could get well under way, the Economic and Social Council of the United Nations met for its regular spring session. Security clearances and other administrative matters had delayed the appointment of a regular U.S. Representative to ECOSOC, so I was tapped for that post.

I will not attempt to give a chronological story of my wanderings in the never-never land of committees, commissions, boards, and councils that make up the Glass House organization. This is not a history of my United Nations service. But I have traveled widely in these regions; I was drafted for all sorts of assignments not normally part of the job of Deputy Representative of the United States to the United Nations. I will never forget, for instance, filling in for the Honorable

Harry Anslinger in the United Nations Commission on Narcotic Drugs for the first two days of the Commission's meeting. These two days taught me two things: first, that it was comparatively easy to be flippant in a United Nations commission, and second, that if you did try flippancy, it might bounce back on you.

Thus, roughly the following dialogue took place between the temporary United States Representative on the United Nations Commission on Narcotic Drugs and a colleague at the end-of-business session the day before Mr. Anslinger was to resume his rightful duties:

WADSWORTH (*mock serious*): There are those among us who have had literally no experience whatever in regard to narcotics. As a purely exploratory project, might it not be appropriate that an arrangement be made to distribute samples of the products which are of concern to the Commission, particularly to those members or temporary members who are not in any way familiar with their use or effect?

COLLEAGUE (*completely deadpan*): The representative of the United States has offered an interesting suggestion, one which might be of considerable value in estimating the effect of various narcotics on the human system. But (*and here he became unusually solemn*), I must warn that the practice of distributing samples might create a dangerous precedent. As an example, the next regularly scheduled meeting of a United Nations commission in this chamber concerns itself with the white-slave traffic!

End of discussion.

Let me illustrate further the variety of my work as United States Representative. One day I would find myself sitting as United States Representative on a committee to draft an agreement on tourism; another day on a committee on the international economic implications of peace; still another on the various pledges of the member governments for expanded technical assistance to what are now known as "developing countries." Later I would find myself working with a committee of hotel proprietors and apartment-house owners in an attempt to overcome difficulties about occupancy of their properties by United Nations representatives.

Other special assignments came my way. In 1955, I was sent to London to represent the United States on the Subcommittee of the United Nations Disarmament Commission. For several sessions, I sat on the Peace Observation Commission with special regard to the Greek-Albanian border situation. Then, in 1956, I was loaned to Washington to head up the United States team that negotiated the International Atomic Energy Agency statute. I went to Vienna in 1957 for the opening session of that agency. In 1958, I was named United States Representative on Disarmament and, in the fall of that year, started the job of negotiating a nuclear test ban treaty in Geneva, where we spent nearly two years in mild frustration. Finally, in September of 1960, I came back to this country to become Chief of Mission and head of the United States Delegation to the General Assembly, winding up my eight-year tour of duty in January, 1961, when the late Adlai E. Stevenson took over.

As I remarked earlier, even this multifaceted career in the United Nations did not give me much opportunity to explore the labyrinth of the Secretariat and the Specialized Agencies and the many other important activities carried on by lesser-known groups. Research for the material in this book has filled out the missing knowledge to a great extent, and I am grateful for the opportunity of learning. I am also grateful for the opportunity of passing on what I have learned, in the hope that I may make more understandable an organization and operation that is much misunderstood and therefore much maligned.

I said at the outset that the coloration of the United Nations' coat is in the eye of the observer, and this is quite legitimate and proper. A citizen of a small country could not be expected to evaluate the United Nations in the same terms as a citizen of the largest country. A Russian must have a concept completely different from that of an American, but this is not due wholly to ideological disagreements, since an American often has a different set of ideas from a Frenchman or an Englishman. Similarly, poorer countries look for things quite different from those sought by richer countries; yet this does not necessarily make any two poor countries more likely to see eye to eye on the United Nations than any two rich countries.

I shall examine the reaction patterns of the various members and member groups, in the hope that once we understand the patterns, some of the exasperation with the United Nations that most of us have felt at one time or another may be put into more nearly logical perspective. I shall discuss national versus international interests, bloc power-politics, the political implications of economic and military pressures, the myths that have grown up, and the propaganda that has helped them grow.

Among other things, I hope to be able to bring increased awareness of the almost incredible amount of good works that are regularly done by lesser-known organs of the Glass House. One rarely hears anything about the United Nations except controversy and crisis. The pounding of a shoe reverberates with a hundred times more decibels than the feeding and care of millions of children, and angry exchanges on colonialism effectively drown out the prayers of thanksgiving arising from millions of newly freed people who have been given better health, hygiene, education, and agricultural techniques.

On the political side, I hope to give some insight into major policy battles: the way the battle lines are drawn, the impulsions and compulsions present at every debate and every vote on a controversial measure. I shall go behind the curtain wherever I cannot lift it entirely, and follow the consultations, the compromises, the prejudices, and *sine qua nons* of the major actors and blocs. The reader will not, I am sure, expect me to be completely dispassionate about all the matters to be discussed, but I do believe that my approach can be characterized as objective, even if not wholly impartial, and such criticism as will be found is intended in good humor and without any lingering antagonisms against people or policies.

For the Glass House is *all* of the United Nations: not only in New York, or Geneva, or Paris, or Rome, or Palestine, or the Congo, but all over the world. Its effect is world-wide. Most people who support it strongly do so for a special reason; a particular aspect is also singled out by those who disapprove. I imagine that there are very few informed people who can say that they thoroughly endorse everything done in and by the Glass House. At the same time, even its most passionate critics have to admit the worth of some of its activities.

After all, this organization is the answer evolved by men of vision to the questions of international cooperation that have plagued mankind throughout recorded history. They tried to take into consideration the weaknesses and shortcomings of the League of Nations, and to avoid them as far as possible. They were not entirely successful, but they did manage to find a formula that holds a solid attraction for the overwhelming majority of all members, as well as for the handful of regimes that are not members. Those who read this book should, if possible, approach it on this basis: that, whether one likes it all or much or little, the concept of the United Nations is inspired by real intellect and deep feeling; that if nations can be persuaded to live reasonably close to its concept, it must be a resounding success; and that even with the bickering and weaknesses already demonstrated, it is still the best existing hope for an ultimate peace with honor and dignity.

Contents

The GLASS HOUSE

1 · The House*

THE OVER-ALL STRUCTURE of the Glass House to some extent parallels that of the League of Nations, but this is largely because the United Nations has retained the European concept of international organization. A major difference is the creation of a small, hard-hitting Security Council for quick response to emergencies with a minimum (at least for this kind of group) of debate. The founding conference in San Francisco in 1945 included a very considerable number of high officials of various governments who had had much experience with the League and who were therefore thoroughly cognizant of that lamented organization's weaknesses as well as strengths. The House's structure, as established in the Charter, is the result of that composite experience.

It is axiomatic that in a voluntary association of a number of independent states, the supreme power of the organization must be conferred upon the major body containing all the members of the association. No matter how many special committees or councils or boards are set up for the expeditious handling of specific subjects, the final responsibility

* For further details on the structure and functioning of the House, the reader is directed to *Basic Facts About the United Nations* (United Nations: Office of Public Information, 1964), to which I am indebted for some of the information in this chapter.

for all actions of the organization must reside in this major body. Thus the General Assembly is the hub of the Glass House, and all the other main and lesser organs radiate out from it. Here are elected all the appropriate members of the other main organs, and here lies the responsibility for the election of all the participants in the lesser organs. Here is the power of the purse-strings, in the making of all appropriations, and the prorating of the budget among the various members.

It is not surprising that when the average citizen thinks of the United Nations, he thinks first of the General Assembly —the body that makes the headlines every year, the sounding board and forum for all the members in putting forward their positions and their arguments. The Security Council has great importance, too, but its ten nonpermanent members—five are designated as permanent members: China, France, the U.S.S.R., the U.K., and the U.S.—are elected by the General Assembly; its recommendations are accepted or rejected by the General Assembly; and in cases where peace is threatened or breached, or aggression has occurred, and the Council cannot, by reason of veto, come to any solid conclusion, the General Assembly can take over the problem under the Uniting for Peace resolution, adopted in November, 1950.

General Assembly. The Assembly itself is not a complicated organization. It has as many members as there are members of the Glass House, and each has one vote, a system similar to the one we in the United States use in our Senate, where each State is allotted 2 votes regardless of its relative size. The first General Assembly, in 1945, reflected the total membership of the Glass House of 50; as this is written, there are 117.

Each Member State is entitled to 5 delegates, and most of them appoint 5 alternates as well. They are appointed in various ways in accordance with the laws and customs of the

THE UNITED NATIONS

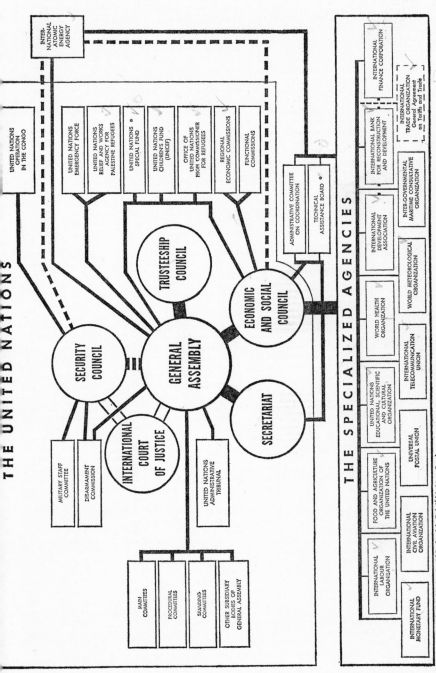

THE SPECIALIZED AGENCIES

*In January, 1966, the United Nations Special Fund and the Technical Assistance Board were consolidated under the name of the United Nations Development Program.

various countries. In the United States, appointments are made by the President with the advice and consent of the Senate. In Great Britain, the Foreign Minister recommends the appointments to the Prime Minister, who makes them without recourse to Parliament. In the Soviet Union, the appointments are made by the Chairman of the Supreme Soviet; in Ghana, by the President.

Delegates are accepted at the General Assembly through the medium of credentials presented to the Secretary General. He will consider the credentials to be in order if they are signed or countersigned by the Chief of State concerned, or if the Chief of State so delegates the authority, the signature of the Foreign Minister or Secretary of State is sufficient.

The Assembly meets annually in New York on the third Tuesday in September, except in years of Presidential elections in the United States. In 1948, the Assembly moved to Paris to escape the campaign hoopla, but since then has taken the less expensive path of remaining in New York and postponing the opening date until after Election Day. Special sessions may be called under certain circumstances but only four have been called since 1945. They were: April, 1947 (on Palestine), April, 1948 (on Palestine), August, 1961 (on Morocco), and May, 1963 (on United Nations financing). In addition, four emergency special sessions have been called: November, 1956 (on Suez), November, 1956 (on Hungary), August, 1956 (on Lebanon), and September, 1960 (on the Congo).

The Assembly's functions may be said to cover virtually all of the problems embodied in the quest for international peace and reduction of tensions. Consequently, there is always the problem of duplication and overlapping with other organs of the U.N., such as the Security Council, and the Assembly is forbidden, as a result, to make recommendations on an issue that is currently being discussed by the Council. Obviously such duplication could be extremely awkward if not dangerous, particularly if an Assembly vote should depart from the line taken by the Council.

The Assembly initiates studies, receives and considers reports from the other organs, makes recommendations, and decides on its own actions to be taken on problems of which it is "seized." It supervises the execution of trusteeship agreements through the Trusteeship Council for all areas not designated as strategic. It elects the ten nonpermanent members of the Security Council, all the members of the Economic and Social Council, the elective members of the Trusteeship Council; and it joins the Security Council in electing the judges of the International Court of Justice and in appointing the Secretary General.

I have mentioned the Uniting for Peace resolution that was adopted by the Assembly in 1950, but I have not adequately stressed its significance to the Glass House as a whole and to the keeping of the peace in particular. Before this resolution was passed, it was possible for any one of the five permanent members of the Security Council to block United Nations action of any kind indefinitely by refusing to support it in the Council. There was no procedure set up by the Charter to allow another organ to take over a problem that was still technically in the purview of the Council.

During the fall of 1950, when the Korean struggle was just warming up into a brisk fire, this same situation arose, and the United Nations was stymied until the Assembly, urged on by the United States and its allies, passed the Uniting for Peace resolution providing that any problem concerning aggression or any threat to the peace could be switched from the Security Council to the Assembly within twenty-four hours of the failure of the Council to act. If the Council sends the matter to the Assembly of its own volition, the Assembly is thereupon "seized" of the question and can proceed to take action on a Uniting for Peace basis. The Soviet Union has never agreed that this procedure is legal, and claims that the Council is the only organ of the United Nations which can order peace-keeping activities or collective action of any kind. This has been their overt reason for refusing to pay for the peace-keeping activities in the Congo and Palestine.

The powers granted to the General Assembly are broader than those of any body I know of in the governmental systems of the world except for the powers held by outright dictators. Certainly no other parliamentary body in an individual state has the right to do all the things that accrue to the Assembly. Other international organizations give similar power to the general conference of their members, but not to the same extent. We have here, therefore, a benign dictatorship wielded by all the members at once rather than by one strong man or even a cabal of powers. The *functions* of the General Assembly, however, carry with them a minimum of naked authority. With very few exceptions, the decisions made by the majority of the nations of the world in the Assembly have no teeth.

As for the mechanics of the General Assembly, a simple majority vote prevails except in what are naïvely termed "important matters," when a two-thirds majority is required. "Important matters" may be proclaimed as such on an *ad hoc* basis, but generally they consist of recommendations on peace and security; election of members to organs; admission, suspension, and expulsion of members; trusteeship questions; and budgetary matters.

Special sessions may be called at the request of the Security Council, of a majority of all the members, or of one or more members with a majority of members concurring. An emergency special session may be called within twenty-four hours of a request by the Security Council or by a majority of all members, as above.

The Assembly functions through seven Main Committees on which all members are entitled to representation. They are:

First Committee (Political and Security, including the regulation of armaments);

Special Political Committee (participates in the activities of the First Committee);

Second Committee (Economic and Financial);

Third Committee (Social, Humanitarian, and Cultural);

Fourth Committee (Trusteeship, including Non-Self-Governing Territories);

Fifth Committee (Administrative and Budgetary); and

Sixth Committee (Legal).

Throughout the session, the General Committee holds frequent meetings in order to oversee the Assembly's operations. This body, which is really a steering committee, is made up of the President and thirteen Vice Presidents of the Assembly and the Chairmen of the seven Main Committees. The Credentials Committee is appointed by the Assembly President at each session to certify the credentials of representatives.

As a general practice, questions on the Assembly's agenda are referred to one of the Main Committees or to a joint committee. In special cases, an *ad hoc* committee may be set up to deal with a specific question. When a committee has formulated its proposals and approved them by a simple majority, they are then submitted to a meeting of the whole Assembly for its approval. A plenary meeting of the Assembly considers those matters that are not referred to a Main Committee or other committee.

In addition, there are two standing committees to aid the Assembly—the Advisory Committee on Administrative and Budgetary Questions and the Committee on Contributions. Committee members are elected by the General Assembly and serve for three years. Two elements determine their selection: the geographic region they represent and their individual merits.

Security Council. The Security Council consists of fifteen members—five of whom are so-called permanent members and are automatically carried over each term, and ten non-permanent members, who are elected for two-year terms on the basis of geographic and political representation. (Until revision of the Charter was ratified in June, 1965, the Council had eleven members—the Big Five and six nonpermanent representatives. The revision was designed to take account of the greatly enlarged membership of the U.N. by increasing Asian and African representation on this body.)

I think the San Francisco conferees in 1945 acted wisely when they arbitrarily named the five then dominant powers as permanent members. In the first place, the great powers belong on the Council: They carry the biggest share of responsibility and should be given commensurate positions of importance. Secondly, the principle of continuity among the membership had to be maintained, particularly since the nonpermanent members are not eligible for immediate re-election. The Council can always count on at least five members who are thoroughly familiar with Council practices and traditions, who are equally familiar with the history of problems that recur from year to year, and at least four of the five who can be counted on to move their powerful weight in the direction of the goal of the greatest good for the United Nations.

These are the five who are entitled to use the "veto," a practice that was adopted in San Francisco because the conferees were unable to agree on any other system of recognition of the comparative importance of the biggest, strongest, richest, and most populous powers. Several formulas of weighted voting were discussed, only to be discarded, and, I think, inevitably. After all, the United States, France, and the United Kingdom could scarcely have allowed the weighting of votes purely on the basis of population, thus giving to China, India, and the Union of Soviet Socialist Republics many more votes than to them. And equally, the less prosperous states would not have wanted to give extra votes to others on the formula of per capita wealth or income. Over and above these perfectly normal and human reactions loomed the danger of adopting any formula that would be subject to change from year to year, causing a veritable mishmash of claim and counterclaim every time the General Assembly met in session.

It was finally decided that the Big Five were entitled to a certain protection against being outvoted in the Security Council, at least, where their very deep interests might be threatened. And so the "veto" came about, and was supported by all of the Five at the Conference. Of course, no one could have guessed, during those halcyon days of 1945, what was going to happen to their precious veto—a veto that they thought would scarcely if ever be used. The box score on the use of vetoes at the end of the 1964/65 session of the Assembly read:

China	1
France	4
U.S.S.R.	103
U.K.	3
U.S.A.	0

China's single veto came in 1955 on the question of admitting Outer Mongolia as a member.

France cast two of its vetoes on the Suez question in 1956, one on the Spanish question in 1946, and one on the second Indonesian case in 1957.

The Soviet Union's vetoes were most heavily used to block admission of new members; fifty of them were cast in such cases. The rest were scattered among political subjects of all kinds, usually Cold War items.

The United Kingdom's vetoes included two when she joined France on the Suez question in 1956, and one on Southern Rhodesia in 1963.

As can be noted, the United States has never used the veto.

One other point should be kept in mind: A negative vote

cast by a permanent member is not considered a veto unless there have been nine or more affirmative votes cast. If less than a majority of the Council has voted in favor of a measure, a negative vote by one of the Five is merely one vote among a majority of dissidents. The United States has cast several of these.

Boiled down to its simplest ingredients, the job of the Security Council is to ward off troubles that might lead to war. It is often used, or misused, by some member trying to blacken the public image of another, but in the main the Council does not allow itself to be deluded by this sort of tactic. In maintaining peace and security, it investigates disputes or "situations" that seem potentially dangerous, recommends methods, and formulates plans to correct the dangerous trend. It may determine the existence of a threat to peace and call on members to apply economic sanctions and other measures short of war to prevent or stop aggression.

On other fronts, it has the responsibility of recommending the admission of new members to the General Assembly, of exercising the trusteeship functions of the United Nations in "strategic areas" (almost never used), and of recommending the appointment of the Secretary General. It also joins the Assembly in the election of the judges of the International Court of Justice.

A vote on all matters other than procedural questions is carried only if it has the approval of nine members, including the five permanent members. If all five permanent members are not included in the nine affirmative votes, a matter fails of passage due to the veto procedure explained above. In procedural matters, the veto does not exist, and any nine affirmative votes are sufficient. Any member who is party to a dispute before the Council must abstain from voting on any resolution bearing on that dispute. The President of the Council is also expected to step down temporarily from the chair if his country is a party to a dispute before the Council. The Presidency rotates alphabetically every month.

While the President of the Council often must preside over extremely tense sessions, his job has its moments of comic relief. During Henry Cabot Lodge's distinguished service as U.S. Representative to the U.N., he had occasion to preside over the Council when Semyon Tsarapkin, then a Deputy to Andrei Vishinsky, had to represent the U.S.S.R. in Vishinsky's absence. In the course of a procedural argument, Tsarapkin called a point of order. Lodge, forgetting that he was in the United Nations rather than in the United States Senate, used the language of the latter body in inquiring: "Will the gentleman state his point of order?"

Tsarapkin, who in a social setting bubbled with humor, immediately became the dedicated defender of his government. Technically correct but perhaps momentarily disoriented by the Capitol Hill phrase, he pounded his desk and snapped: "I am not the gentleman! I am the representative of the U.S.S.R.!"

Instantly, amid the roar of laughter, Lodge shot back: "Surely the two are not mutually exclusive?"

As can be seen, the Council differs sharply from the General Assembly in functions, scope, specific powers, and tasks. Except for the election of new members and of the judges of the International Court of Justice, and the appointment of the Secretary General, in which it functions as an organ of checks and balances; peace is the Council's main business. It pays no attention to budgets and administrative matters; it has no responsibility in the economic and social field; it has no part in the deliberations of the main committees of the Glass House. It is so constituted that it can and often does leap into action on only a few hours' notice; members belonging to the Council must always have a qualified person ready to sit at any hour 365 days per year. It can and often does call before it witnesses from United Nations members who are not members of the Council; occasionally, it will hear representatives of states not members of the United Nations at all.

Throughout its history, the Council has consisted of the ablest men of their time in their respective countries. One does not "send a boy to do a man's job" in that body. As a general rule, the permanent representative of his country sits on the Council. Occasionally, a Foreign Minister or Secretary of State will appear on unusually important cases, but this is not standard procedure. Accordingly, the United States has been represented in the Council by such as Warren Austin, Ernest Gross, Henry Cabot Lodge, and Adlai Stevenson; I also sat in for a few months in late 1960. The British representatives have included Sir Gladwyn Jebb, Selwyn Lloyd, Anthony Nutting, Sir Pierson Dixon, and Sir Patrick Dean. The Russians have included Jacob Malik, Andrei Vishinsky, Andrei Gromyko, and Valerian Zorin.

It is somewhat surprising and at the same time reassuring to find that this august body has had to make a minimum of really difficult and far-reaching decisions in regard to action. Often it has sufficed for the Council to meet and hear the complaints and countercharges, giving them the exposure needed for better understanding. Many times the Council merely notes the complaint and the answer, calls on the parties to refrain from provocative acts, and subsides quietly but watchfully, having been "seized" of the problem and having said, "Go, and sin no more." This is not to say that there have been no violent altercations, no bitter recriminations, no Cold War extensions in the Council chamber. Far from it. But the fact remains that only once—in the Korean case—has there been a peace-keeping operation involving collective military action of an active, shooting-war nature. This occurred because of the walk-out staged by the Soviet Union, a mistake it is unlikely to repeat in such a situation. All the other cases that required United Nations forces were handled by putting United Nations people in the field under United Nations command, with orders not to shoot unless it was impossible to withhold fire for their own safety.

Thus the Kashmir case required only thirty-five military observers, mingling with the Indian and Pakistani troops on both sides of the border. Since the undeclared war of the summer of 1965, the number of observers has been understandably large, particularly since neither side has shown much desire to live up to the cease-fire brought about by the U.N. If the cease-fire could be followed by a political agreement, all the observers could be withdrawn.

In the various crises in the Middle East, the military observers have not been called upon to shoot. The United Nations Emergency Force in the Suez case were peace-keepers in the real sense of the word. In Yemen and West Irian, the operation was tiny and pacific, with the parties paying the expense. In the Congo, however, the difficulties were immense, and although the United Nations Operations in the Congo rarely had to fight for their lives, the general instability of the situation was most frustrating.

The Cyprus case is still giving a great deal of trouble and may yet turn out to be a United Nations failure. Here, both sides in the struggle have been doing their best to circumvent the United Nations peace force, and have been bent on each other's destruction in spite of lip service paid to cease-fire demands of the Security Council. It is not so much a matter of the United Nations men being resented or distrusted as it is a matter of their being ignored to the fullest possible extent. Hate is the real ruler of Cyprus.

On the non-peace-keeping side, perhaps the most notable action of the Council came in 1955 at the time of the breaking of the impasse over new membership in the Glass House. After a long, elaborate, and tortuous series of conferences among the Five, a large number of states that had been knocking futilely on the door were surprised and pleased when it was swung suddenly open for sixteen of them. These were: Albania, Austria, Jordan, Ireland, Portugal, Hungary, Italy, Romania, Bulgaria, Finland, Ceylon, Nepal, Libya, Cambodia, Laos, and Spain. In fact, of all the states considered to be interested in admission at that time, the only unsuccessful ones were Japan, Red China, Outer Mongolia, and the divided states of Germany, Korea, and Vietnam. Japan was admitted the following year, while Outer Mongolia was finally admitted in 1961, together with Mauritania. The soothsayers tell us that Red China may be successful within "a few years," but there is no telling about the divided states—the impasses are such that unification may have to come about before the Cold War relaxes its grip on these.

Economic and Social Council. The Economic and Social Council consists of twenty-seven members, elected by the General Assembly in staggered groups, each group for a different three-year term. (Like the Security Council, ECOSOC's membership was enlarged—from its original eighteen—when Charter revisions were approved in June, 1965.) ECOSOC members are entitled to immediate re-election and, in practice, quite a few of them are so designated. The five permanent members of the Security Council are also (although non-officially) permanent members of ECOSOC. Other comparatively large countries, such as India, are almost invariably listed among the membership, and members of other geographic groups, such as Latin America, East and West Europe, and the Afro-Asians, usually hold several seats. These last are subject to intragroup rotation by agreement among themselves.

This particular Council leads a life of sheltered anonymity most of the time, and its responsibilities and functions do not as a rule produce headlines. It is in charge of the economic and social programs of the United Nations; it makes studies, reports, and recommendations on all matters appropriate to the functions. It seeks to promote respect for and observance of human rights and fundamental freedoms for all, and with indifferent success. It calls conferences and prepares draft conventions for submission to the General Assembly, negotiates agreements with Specialized Agencies on their relationship with the United Nations, coordinates the activities of these agencies by means of recommendations to them and to the General Assembly, and consults with nongovernmental organizations on matters of mutual concern and responsibility.

Its accomplishments have been significant in the aggregate, although few have been singled out for heavy attention. On the plus side may be counted the Convention on Human Rights, the Convention on the Status of Women, the creation and encouragement of the regional economic commissions, and the functional commissions.

Just as important, if not more so, have been the constant consultations with nongovernmental organizations, who are accredited to and associated with ECOSOC in two categories: Category A, which consists of those organizations having strong associations with the Council and its work, and Category B, those associations that have a basic interest in most of the activities of the Council and its commissions. Category A includes only ten groups: International Chamber of Commerce, International Confederation of Free Trade Unions, International Cooperative Alliance, International Federation of Agricultural Producers, International Federation of Christian Trade Unions, International Organization of Employers, Inter-Parliamentary Union, World Federation of Trade Unions, World Federation of United Nations Associations, and World Veterans Federation. Category B, comprising more than 130 organizations, lists such groups as: All African Women's Conference, CARE, European Alliance of Press Agencies, International Automobile Federation, League of Red Cross Societies, Lions International, National Association of Manufacturers, Rotary International, The Salvation Army, World Federation for Mental Health, and World's Young Women's Christian Association. Finally, there exists a

Register containing the names of more than 200 groups, which have the right of occasional *ad hoc* consultations with the Secretary General.

The value of these nongovernmental organizations is that they are composed of people who are close to the problems being studied and attacked by the Council and by its two main subsidiary bodies: the Economic Commission and the Social Commission. Their membership represents a cross section of the general public of many countries, and their reaction to proposed plans and programs can be invaluable to international officials who could not be expected to know the scope of such a broad spectrum of public opinion in advance.

The Category A nongovernmental organizations have the right to speak at ECOSOC meetings, putting forward their positions in regard to subjects before the Council and proposing items for the agenda. Category B nongovernmental organizations may submit written statements for circulation as documents among the appropriate United Nations bodies.

Trusteeship Council. The Trusteeship Council is composed of several types of members. (1) Members of the United Nations administering Trust Territories: Australia, Belgium, France, Italy, New Zealand, the United Kingdom, and the United States; (2) permanent members of the Security Council who do not administer Trust Territories: China and the U.S.S.R.; and (3) six other members elected by the General Assembly for three-year terms, in order to make an equal division (8 to 8) of administering countries and nonadministering countries. Elected members are eligible for immediate re-election upon expiration of their terms.

The function of the Council is, broadly, to look after the well-being of all the Trust Territories, expedite their emergence into independence where this is possible, provide for annual reports from the administering authorities, examine and discuss them at hearings where representatives from the Trust Territories may be heard, and take petitions from the populace of various territories under consideration. In oversimplified terms, the job of the Trusteeship Council is to work itself out of a job. How well it has succeeded can be shown by a few simple statistics. When the Council first took over in March, 1947, there were ten so called Trust Territories:

Cameroons (France)	Tanganyika (U.K.)
Cameroons (U.K.)	Western Samoa (New Zealand)
Togoland (France)	New Guinea (Australia)
Togoland (U.K.)	Nauru (Australia, New Zealand, U.K.)
Ruanda-Urundi (Belgium)	Pacific Islands (U.S.)

Somaliland (Italy)—added in 1949

Today, all but three of these—Nauru, New Guinea, and the Pacific Islands, which are composed of the Marshalls, Marianas, and Carolines—have attained independence. Due to their far-scattered territory and sparse population and wealth, the island territories have been the most difficult to plan for, and the development of the Papuans in New Guinea is such that self-government is not yet a practical matter. Efforts are being made all along the line to lead these territories toward a greater degree of self-government, but it has been and will continue to be a slow business. At the same time, we must applaud the fact that since 1955, when British Togoland became the first of the group to emerge from trusteeship to independence, areas totaling approximately 1,000,000 square miles and populations totaling more than 29,000,000 have become self-governing under this system.

Non-self-governing territories are usually not as ripe for independence as are the Trust Territories. As a rule, they are far smaller, and less likely to be viable states on their own. The United Nations feels sure that some of them will attain complete sovereignty, while others will form free associations or federations with neighbors. The latter alternative is considered to be the best prospect for most of the group, and plans for such regional associations are being urged on the administering countries. This is not a simple matter, however, because the guiding principle is that of self-determination, and it would not always be wise for an administering country to urge a specific course on its colonies, lest there be accusations of undue influence.

International Court of Justice. The International Court of Justice is located at The Hague, and is the principal judicial body of the United Nations. One of the primary organs originally set up by the League of Nations, it has inherited to a real extent the League's mantle of respect. The traditions of the Court were created under the aegis of the League, and it has also reflected from the first the whole body of European juridical precedent. This last seems to have outweighed whatever Eastern juridical concepts might have been introduced following the election of such outstanding Asian jurists as Sir Muhammad Zafrulla Khan of Pakistan.

The Court receives or accepts cases from parties to the Court Statute, from other states under conditions imposed by the Security Council, or from the Security Council itself. The General Assembly and the Council can ask the Court for an advisory opinion on any legal question; other organs of the United Nations and the Specialized Agencies may seek advisory opinions on matters arising in connection with their functions.

The Court relies on varied bodies of law in arriving at decisions: international conventions setting up rules recognized by the contesting states, international custom as evidence of general usage accepted as law, and general principles of law as recognized by most nations. There are fifteen judges, elected separately but concurrently by the Security Council and the General Assembly.

Due to the hesitancy of some of the great powers, including the United States, the International Court of Justice has not been confronted with many decisions of real import, except for a few advisory opinions that have had far-reaching consequences. The United States Senate, in ratifying or giving "advice and consent" on the Charter of the United Nations and the Statute of the Court, adopted a reservation, known as the Connally Reservation after its author, Senator Tom Connally of Texas. This amendment to the ratification and participation act provides that the United States may deny the Court's jurisdiction in any matters where the United States is one of the parties, if it seems in our interest to do so. In other words, we will go before the Court only if we want to.

In spite of this and other roadblocks to the Court's full assumption of responsibility, there is no doubt as to the esteem in which it is held all over the world. Membership is much desired, and its judges are respected and admired for their learning and dignity. They serve a nine-year term and may be re-elected, and they are not allowed to engage in any other occupation during their term of office.

The most recent action of note was the advisory opinion handed down July 20, 1962, to the effect that the cost of peace-keeping operations was properly a part of the budget of the United Nations. This meant that members failing to pay such costs were subject to the provisions of Article 19 of the Charter. Since there is considerable confusion about this part of the Charter, particularly in the light of Soviet refusal to pay peace-keeping costs, I want to quote it:

> A member of the United Nations which is in arrears in the payment of its financial contributions to the Organization *shall have no vote in the General Assembly* if the amount of its arrears equals or exceeds the amount of the contributions due from it for the preceding two full years. The General Assembly may, nevertheless, permit such a member to vote if it is satisfied that the failure to pay is due to conditions beyond the control of the Member [italics added].

I shall discuss the political implications of this situation in more detail in a subsequent chapter, but I quote the passage here so that the full implications of the advisory opinion can be understood. Other decisions, moving back through the years, include the Cambodia-Thailand case of June, 1962, which resolved an ownership dispute over a piece of land between the two countries; the Honduras-Nicaragua case of 1960, also a border-strip jurisdictional decision; the Swiss-United States so-called Interhandel case of 1959, which finally was ordered back to mediation and successfully concluded by negotiation; and the Morocco case of 1952 between France and the United States, in which the question of the jurisdiction of the Court was raised again, this time by the French.

Secretariat. The Secretariat is the staff of the United Nations. This also follows the European concept of international organization as well as national organization. Most of the major subdivisions of the various European governments, particularly the Foreign Office, have a Secretary General or a Secretariat to carry on the administrative and other staff work for that particular body. Recently the term has been adopted in a limited sense to describe certain functions in the United States White House and State Department organizations. For the United Nations, it is one of the main organs of the House, headed by a Secretary General appointed by the General Assembly on the recommendation of the Security Council.

Three men have held the job: Trygve Lie of Norway, Dag Hammarskjöld of Sweden, and U Thant of Burma. As can be readily understood, one of the main requirements of the job is courage, and all three Secretaries have possessed this attribute to an unusual degree. The Charter gives the Secretary General certain guidelines of function and responsibility, but the man himself builds the job and creates the image that the world comes to know. Trygve Lie was called upon to do only a fairly routine job during his first five-year term. This is not to say that the job of building the organization, the buildings, and the diplomatic precedents was simple and easy —it is merely that the most difficult situations arose later.

Probably Mr. Lie will be remembered most widely for his devoted support and attention to the Korean problem—a devotion that actually cost him the last year or two of his job. He accepted the mandate of the Security Council and the General Assembly to prosecute the collective action against North Korea and thereby won the undying enmity of the Soviet Union and its satellites. Dag Hammarskjöld's death is still so recent that few will have forgotten his own special brand of courage. Perhaps his finest hour was the speech he made during the Assembly session of 1960—the famous shoe-pounding session—in answer to Premier Khrushchev's demand that he resign because of his "handling" of the Congo situation.

U Thant has displayed the same sort of calm courage as his predecessors. The first Asian to hold the post after two Scandinavian experts, he quickly established his image as an imperturbable, wholly devoted, scrupulously nonaligned international civil servant who shrinks from nothing and sometimes uses rather earthy expressions to reveal his feelings, as witness his exclamation that the top officials of a certain troubled country were just "a bunch of clowns!" During the summer of 1964, he made a trip to the Soviet Union to talk about, among other things, Soviet refusal to pay for peace-keeping. In spite of the fact that he got no encouragement from Khrushchev and company, U Thant made a television broadcast in Moscow, crisply told the Russian people how mistaken their government was in this matter, and warned that the possible collapse of the United Nations due to this position would be laid squarely at the Soviet door.

One of the best ways of judging the job and the men who have made it is through the eyes of the top people of the various member powers, both large and small. In the early days of 1945 to 1950, the position was considered important, but comparatively far down the list in protocol honor. Trygve Lie, and in fact Dag Hammarskjöld in the early years of his term, often writhed inwardly to find themselves so far "below the salt" at official functions in national capitals. Gradually, however, a strong trend developed toward reassessing the comparative importance of the post, and by the tragic end of Hammarskjöld's term of office, he was received all over the world with the veritable red-carpet treatment. U Thant is also welcomed like a chief of state wherever he goes, and the honors accorded to the position of Secretary General are impressive indeed.

Not only the honors, but the job and its functions have moved in a most healthful direction. I rather doubt that the United States originally visualized such a powerful person in 1945, but as matters progressed, and it became obvious that because of the Cold War we could not expect the world always to take our position as the last word, the nonaligned person of the Secretary General could do a better job with many countries than we could because he had no political ax to grind. More than once during my tenure in New York, the Secretary General pointedly let the United States know that certain chickens were coming home to roost and certain home truths had to be assimilated. The fact is that although the Soviet Union often accused Hammarskjöld of being "oriented to the West," the West was regularly the recipient of friendly but unmistakable criticism from him. I have not served with U Thant since he has been Secretary General, but I knew him well as Burma's Permanent Representative and I have no doubt that he would not hesitate to "lay it on the line" with us, as did his predecessors.

All in all, then, the Secretary General's job has developed through the characters and creeds of its incumbents, and the world is far better off than we have any right to expect because of it. When the Secretary General of the United Nations takes charge, even the mutual hatred between Arab and Israeli or Greek and Turkish Cypriots seems held in abeyance, even if only temporarily. The Secretary General speaks, and the world listens.

Something of the importance of the Secretary General's job was underscored by the difficulty encountered in making selections when the term expired. On both occasions, in March and April of 1953 and in October of 1961, discussions among the five permanent members of the Security Council were extremely protracted and often frustrating. In 1953, we were seeking a successor to Trygve Lie. Four out of the five permanent members were friendly to Lie, but we knew that the Soviets would never support him, so we sought elsewhere for a compromise candidate. Such a person would obviously have to come from a neutral or not heavily aligned country, and for at least ten days there was a complete impasse.

My recollection is that the French originally came up with the name of Hammarskjöld, who, though well and favorably known as a diplomat and administrator in his native Sweden, had less reputation in the international community. His resources, experience, and reputation, however, were detailed to the governments of the Five, and after some unnecessary delay, unanimous approval resulted. He later told me that he had been utterly amazed by the consensus—his entire philosophy of international life was so clearly opposed to Communism that he had been convinced that the Soviets would have to oppose him.

In 1961, when U Thant came into the picture, the Soviet "troika" proposition was still being pressed. In this case, the Soviets were not necessarily opposed to him because of anything he had said or done—they were opposed to any single man being vested with such power. As I shall discuss in a subsequent chapter, the Soviets simply could not and would not believe that any human being could be truly neutral, and they therefore sought to protect their own point of view with a three-man Secretary Generalship, one representing the "West," one the "East," and the third a neutral posture. Each was to have a veto over the votes of the other two.

Let us draw a merciful curtain over the campaign to sell

the troika, and content ourselves with the simple statement that U Thant convinced both East and West that he could in fact be neutral (which he has been), and that the U.S.S.R. withdrew the troika proposal in the clear light of overwhelming opposition to it from virtually every quarter. U Thant did not have to seek support from most of the members of the United Nations. The United States, United Kingdom, France, and many others took the initiative in letting it be known that he would be satisfactory to them, and thereafter sat quietly by and allowed Asian and African members to campaign for him with the Soviet bloc. That they were successful would again indicate that the Soviet Union and its friends are far from turning a deaf ear when there seems to be a strong ground swell in favor of a candidacy or a policy.

An international staff of some 6,000 assists the Secretary General, with something approaching 4,000 being headquartered at the Glass House in New York. The rest are scattered in posts and missions all over the world, with the next largest group centered in Geneva at the Palais des Nations. The ebb and flow of Secretariat personnel around the world is such that statistical precision is most difficult, and I will not attempt a listing of their population by country where assigned. Suffice it to say that more than 500 are chosen because of special language requirements, more than 100 are chosen for specific services, nearly 200 work for the Technical Assistance Board, more than 400 are classified as Field Service. The rest of the Secretariat staff consists of administrative personnel, as well as clerical and manual workers.

It can thus be seen that there is much more to the Secretariat job than merely routine, day-to-day housekeeping. Experts in virtually every conceivable line of endeavor are found in the Technical Assistance Board and the Field Service. Library work and public-relations work are carried on in the United Nations Information Service centers all over the world.

One significant rule has been in force from the very outset

of the United Nations' life: The Secretary General and his staff must not seek or receive instructions from any government or other authority outside the Glass House, and all members must agree to respect the exclusively international character of the Secretariat and must promise not to seek to influence it in carrying out its responsibilities.

In this connection, we may recall one of the relatively rare cases in which the Secretary General, in 1953, dismissed employees for conduct prejudicial to effective performance of duty. The twenty-one who had been dismissed appealed to the U.N. Administrative Tribunal, which was set up in 1949 to act as a "court of appeals" for U.N. employees who feel aggrieved at some disciplinary action taken against them or feel that their talents have not been recognized by advancement, promotion, or transfer. In the 1953 case, the discharged Secretariat personnel requested reinstatement with back pay and damages. There was considerable documented connection with Communist activities, and seventeen of the accused had invoked the Fifth Amendment when questioned. The Tribunal backed the Secretary General in ten of the cases, holding them to have been proper dismissals for cause, but found in favor of the other eleven, at least to the extent of back pay and damages. The Secretary General has an option, which he at that time exercised, to refuse to reinstate, but the indemnities ordered amounted to nearly $180,000.

This raised a frightful storm all over the United States, generated by people who believed all twenty-one employees to be equally guilty. The fact that all twenty-one were of United States nationality did not help. Soon the U.S. Congress took up the matter and, after heated debate, passed a resolution to the effect that if the indemnities had to be paid (and they did), they would have to be financed from sources of income other than "funds heretofore or hereafter appropriated by the United States Congress." Our delegation was successful in carrying this point with Mr. Hammarskjöld, who found the funds in such a way that the United States appropriation was not involved. Later, the United Nations made arrangements establishing a special fund for such purposes with money from the staff-assessment scheme, which is the internal tax that United Nations employees pay in lieu of national taxes.

As the foregoing incident shows, not all Secretariat personnel or all member states have been lily-white in observance of the rule against influencing Secretariat activities, but in the main the members of the Secretariat staff are devoted international civil servants and are respected as such by all concerned.

It is of course standard procedure to tell the Secretary General and his top staff of the policy of one's country via strictly diplomatic channels. Upon receiving word from his Foreign Minister or Secretary of State, the Permanent Representative seeks an appointment with the Secretary General. At such a meeting, the Representative states that he has received instructions from his government to approach the Secretary General and tell him that his government feels strongly that the United Nations should take such and such a position on this and that question. The Secretary General graciously (usually—sometimes he is annoyed!) receives the information and tells the Representative to thank his government for keeping him informed as to its policy, also to report that this approach will be officially noted and placed in the file with the other statements of policy he has received on the subject. After this, if they have known each other long enough and well enough, they may have some informal conversation about the matter within the limits of what the Secretary General is willing to have reported. On some occasions, the Secretary General may even indicate his agreement with the reported position. Since my experience was exclusively with Mr. Hammarskjöld in these matters, I can report that he, at least, did not hesitate to express strong disagreement with the United States policy whenever he felt it, which was not often. I imagine that U Thant is equally candid with those he knows reasonably well, and Trygve Lie had a wide reputation for bluntness on these occasions.

The Secretariat structure consists of: the Office of the Secretary General, which includes the Office of Legal Affairs, the Controller, and the Office of Personnel; two Under Secretaries for Special Political Affairs (usually a Russian and an American); the Departments of Political and Security Council Affairs, Economic and Social Affairs, and Trusteeship and Information from Non-Self-Governing Territories; the Offices of Public Information, Conference Services, and General Services.

Peace-Keeping Activities. These activities are, of course, separate and apart from the regular organs of the United Nations, but the chart on page 5 shows them as part of the radiating activities attached to the core of the structure. Now that the U.N. military force has been withdrawn from the Congo, the only truly active peace-keeping operations are those in Palestine and in Cyprus. The U.N. Congo operation continues in a nonmilitary sense, and in various other places, such as northern Palestine, there are United Nations "presences," which means small observer teams.

The United Nations Emergency Force (UNEF) was first created by the General Assembly in 1956, but the need for help in the Middle East area started long before then.

The Secretary General has said—in discussing the continual state of unrest in the Middle East—"there is a general consensus everywhere that, but for the United Nations, that area of the world would have long been a scene of ugly clashes perhaps developing into wider entanglements."

The adoption of the Palestine partition plan by the General Assembly in November, 1947, was followed by fighting between Israel and the Arab states; it continued after the state of Israel was established, in May, 1948, and was finally terminated by a United Nations cease-fire. A United Nations mediator guided the armistice agreements that were signed in

1949 by Israel and four Arab countries: Egypt, Jordan, Lebanon, and Syria. Under these agreements, mixed armistice commissions were set up to check on the working of the agreements, and a United Nations Truce Supervision Organization was formed, with a chief of staff and international military observers headquartered in Jerusalem. The military observers investigate complaints of armistice violations and report, as the need arises, to the Security Council.

Tension has not been reduced, and border incidents occur frequently. In 1956, the Suez crisis was resolved by agreement on the withdrawal of Israeli, British, and French forces from Egyptian territory and the establishment of UNEF to prevent further fighting. The Suez Canal, blocked temporarily as a result of the crisis, was reopened by the United Nations. UNEF was assembled within forty-eight hours, to become the world's first truly international force. By patrolling the Egyptian-Israeli armistice demarcation line and the international frontier to the south of the Gaza Strip, it has brought calm to this tension-ridden region. Other aspects under dispute are being handled by other United Nations organs.

The Conciliation Commission for Palestine, since its establishment in 1948, has directed its efforts to help the disputing parties achieve a final settlement on all questions. The Conciliation Commission—composed of representatives of France, Turkey, and the United States—also dealt with the Arab refugees who left Palestine at the time of the fighting there in 1948. The commission is now dormant, having virtually no functions.

United Nations Operations in the Congo (ONUC, from its initials in French) came into being shortly after that Belgian colony won its independence, in July of 1960. The Congolese Government soon had to cope with a massive array of problems: Skilled foreign personnel left the country in droves, while internal rebellions in the army ranks and attacks on

Europeans sowed widespread terror and anarchy. Belgium's quick dispatch of metropolitan troops to safeguard the beleaguered Europeans only compounded the disorder. When the Congolese Government requested military aid from the U.N. to defend its national territory against external aggression, United Nations troops were supplied by the neutral powers, including Asian and African states; they arrived in the Congo on July 14.

The purposes of the United Nations in this operation were set forth by the Security Council in a series of resolutions.

To help the Congolese Government restore and maintain the national unity and territorial integrity of the Congo.

To help the Government restore and maintain law and order throughout the country.

To protect the country from civil war and to help the Government control and pacify tribal conflicts.

To protect the country from outside interference in its internal affairs, particularly through the elimination of non-Congolese mercenaries.

To help the Congolese Government develop and maintain essential public services, and to assist it through a wide and long-term program of training and technical assistance.

A substantial investment in manpower was needed to accomplish this undertaking. At times, the force ONUC had at its disposal numbered more than 20,000 officers and men, in addition to some 1,300 civilians.

Finally, the Secretary General reported in February, 1963, that the political independence of the Congo had been preserved and that it had regained its territorial integrity. The gravest threat to the territorial integrity of the Congo, the secessionist activities of the leaders of Katanga Province, had been terminated. The Secretary General warned, however, that "given an absence of alertness or a too rapid withdrawal of the ONUC troops," the Katangese problem must recur. Consequently, United Nations troops remained in the Congo until June, 1964, because of the continuing need of the Congolese Government for United Nations military assistance in restoring law and order, particularly because of the menace of tribal clashes. The force was, however, scaled down progressively.

As the U.N.'s role in active military operations subsided, emphasis shifted to civilian assistance and reconstruction of the Congo. These aspects had formed part of the United Nations operation from the beginning, and a special Congo Fund had been created, supported by voluntary contributions from various governments. For 1963, a $19-million civilian-assistance program was scheduled, provided funds were available. This has been the largest single program of civil aid the United Nations has ever launched.

Through this program, and at the request of the government, more than 1,000 international experts are working in every sector of the Congo's life, from agriculture to social welfare. Furthermore, the United Nations is helping to guarantee maintenance of essential services in years to come by training Congolese nationals to qualify for these vital positions.

Although the military ONUC force was withdrawn on June 30, 1964, the future of that unfortunate country remains uncertain. All the world, I imagine, recognizes that one of the major difficulties was and is the premature winning of independence without preparation except in the most simple matters. Add to this the heritage of untamed tribal hatreds, the petty jealousies in the leadership, and the total unreadiness of the vast numbers of its ordinary citizens for democratic responsibility, and we must indeed wonder that they have done as well as they have.

It will be noted that virtually all the troops recruited for the Congo were Asians and Africans, and that the few white contingents were from Sweden, Ireland, or other neutral countries. This is in line with the realistic decision to make sure that no troops would appear on the scene from any country which could possibly have an ax to grind; and also the realization that the Congolese people, just emerging from colonial rule under the Belgians, would cooperate more easily with nonwhite troops, considering them more sympathetic to their cause.

Ever since the troops were withdrawn, there have been various groups of "rebels" waging guerrilla warfare in various parts of the Congo. The newspapers and the Congolese Government refer to some of these as Communist-led and -inspired, particularly from the Peking side of the Communist camp. As is the case in nearly every country where guerrillas operate, these irregulars have enjoyed considerable, although spotty, success. In a country such as the Congo, or Vietnam, the central government simply cannot generate enough support among the people in the far-flung provinces to hold the rebels down. A huge percentage of the effort of the Leopoldville government must, as a result, be diverted away from campaigns to achieve a viable economy and into military-political campaigns to preserve the very existence of the government.

By the end of 1964, it was obvious that the recall of Moïse Tshombe did not provide the whole answer. This is partly because Mr. Tshombe had little or no strength politically outside of Katanga before he went into self-imposed exile, and as I shall point out later, he was not even sure of a popular majority in his own province. How such an individual could be expected to pull the Congo together is hard to visualize. He apparently claimed good relations with the rebel groups, but did not realize that such relations were good mostly because he was a rebel against Leopoldville himself. When he became Leopoldville incarnate, his former friends turned on him, which he and President Kasavubu might have expected. Despite his dismissal in the fall of 1965, Mr. Tshombe seems to retain a fairly strong political position.

Two activities that have to do with refugee relief and welfare activities are pinpointed on the chart on page 5. The first, the United Nations High Commissioner for Refugees, is a somewhat all-embracing function that provides care for people who are homeless as a result of wars and other conflicts. This does not include the Arab refugees, who are the concern of the second organization. The chief instrument of the High Commissioner is the 1951 convention relating to the status of refugees, which defines minimum rights for such people. At present, the office provides material help and relocation for refugees in Europe and the Far East, and to scattered groups in the Middle East.

In North Africa, working jointly with the League of Red Cross Societies, the United Nations High Commissioner for Refugees provided food and shelter to refugees from Algeria in Tunisia and Morocco, assisted their repatriation, and helped re-establish them in Algeria. Many hundreds of thousands have been helped in Hong Kong and Macao, fleeing from Chinese Communism. Many thousands more from Tibet, Rwanda, Hungary, Cuba, and Vietnam have been aided, the total of all refugees coming to well over a million persons.

The United Nations Relief and Works Agency (UNRWA) deals exclusively with Arab refugees who fled from Palestine in 1948. As of June 14, 1965, the agency still had a roster of more than a million refugees—half of them under the age of eighteen. It started operations in 1950, financed by voluntary contributions, and its present mandate expires on June 30, 1966. In cooperation with the host governments—Jordan, Lebanon, Syria, and the United Arab Republic—the agency carries out its twofold tasks: The immediate ones are to provide food, health services, education, training, and shelter for the refugees. The long-term goal is to help them become self-supporting through vocational and teacher training.

According to UNRWA reports, the refugees remain determined to be repatriated to their homeland, and the Arab states back their demands. Israel's position, however, is that repatriation would constitute a threat to its security and is out of the question.

We have now covered the six "main organs" of the Glass House and two of the activities that belong to the General Assembly, at least in the official chart of the organization. The chapters that follow describe the functions of various organizations that owe their existence and continued operation to at least one of the six main organs.

It is not difficult to assess the problems that faced the organizers of the Glass House in the building of the structure itself. Member states could be counted on to put forward pet ideas, some of them duplicating already existing services, at least in part. Other members, particularly the less wealthy ones, continually worked to establish systems whereby a world-wide "share the wealth" program would take from the rich and give to the poor. The Communist states worked unremittingly, and are still working, for structural changes that will give them a virtual veto over anything they don't like. My hat is off to the members who have stood firm and have given the world an organization that is strong enough to survive and flexible enough to please a huge majority of its members.

2 · War Against the Causes of War: The U.N. Combat Team

In TALKING WITH people around the country, I have found, not to my surprise but to my definite disappointment, that a very large percentage of them are unaware of the scope of the work done by the Specialized Agencies of the Glass House and the other affiliated organizations of the United Nations family. I say "not to my surprise" because, as I have observed earlier, the world's headlines are accorded to the troublemakers rather than to the peacemakers. There is little "news" in the painstaking studies of water resources for irrigation and electric-power potential in a developing country. There is no "news" in the successful training of a national finance-planning staff for an Asian country that was sorely lacking in this regard or in the hundreds of successful projects in the fields of public health, education, agriculture, communications, transportation, and civil-service training.

Yet these operations make up the major fronts of the "War Against the Causes of War"—a relentless series of campaigns against poverty, hunger, disease, and ignorance. These are the armies, if you will, which not only know where all these enemies of mankind live and thrive, but which in their quiet way are doing something about it within the limits of their often inadequate appropriations. For they know—as most of us merely suspect—that in these times a people with a reasonably

36

good standard of living have a far better chance to survive in viable independence than a people cowering under the hoofs of the modern Four Horsemen mentioned above. The poor man, the hungry man, the sick man, and the illiterate man make up the populations who are ripe for the "isms" that often lead to war. These are the easily inflamed, often downtrodden, miserable-mind-in-miserable-bodies sort of people who tend to follow the demagogue and the revolutionary in a blind search for betterment.

I do not mean, of course, that aggression and warlike proclivities and vaulting ambition reside only in the downtrodden. Most of the major aggressor nations of the twentieth century had a standard of living well above the world average. But in modern times, with nuclear weapons, fantastic delivery systems, space operations, and all the rest, it is beginning to look as though the larger, more powerful, and richer nations are coming to the realization that mutual destruction through all-out war is merely one way, and a particularly messy way, of committing suicide. Therefore, they are groping for some kind of coexistence that will save the face of their own kind of "ism," and they are being careful, especially since the Cuban missile crisis of 1962, not to allow their politico-ideological differences to draw them down the slippery slope toward reciprocal annihilation.

One finds, therefore, that bellicosity is largely being isolated in various parts of the world that have been underdeveloped, and where the downtrodden can still be roused to fighting pitch by slogans and platforms promising their betterment. South America, Africa, Asia—these are the places where, in large measure, the simplest causes of the simplest wars still reside. It is in these areas that the Glass House, through the organs that are charged with these duties, plies its patient trade of improving living standards by multilateral cooperative action, and it is well worth our time to understand what is going on and how it is being done.

A basic purpose of the United Nations, enshrined in the Charter, is to promote economic and social progress and development for all, thus reinforcing another primary purpose, the maintenance of international peace and security. In recent years, the General Assembly has devoted an increasing amount of attention to problems of economic development. This is only to be expected, because, since the admission of the new African states, the great majority of the Assembly's present members are poor countries. In terms of natural resources, many of these so-called underdeveloped or developing countries are potentially wealthy, but in terms of per capita income, living standards, and industry, a great gap separates them from the countries of Western Europe, North America, and even the Soviet bloc. These "poor" countries are politically as disputatious as their "rich" cousins—they are, after all, composed of human beings, and, as Aristotle pointed out, man is a political animal. But, I believe, over the years, they have been less inclined than their rich cousins to envisage world problems in ideological terms. They have their own war to wage, and it is not an ideological one. It is the war against poverty.

One of the three councils of the U.N. is specifically concerned with the "War Against the Causes of War." This is the Economic and Social Council, whose newly enlarged membership of twenty-seven reflects even more now than in the past the interests and views of the "have" and "have-not" nations alike. If the richest countries have had a somewhat disproportionate role in ECOSOC, it is because they, after all, put up most of the money that goes into the U.N.'s development operations. But the rules of ECOSOC contain no "veto" or other big-power strangle hold, and in deliberations the rich countries can always be outvoted by the poor. Moreover, ECOSOC's composition reflects the spirit that underlies all U.N. aid programs: cooperation on terms as nearly equal as possible between those who give and those who receive. U.N. aid is never forced down a country's throat. Rather, the developing countries themselves help decide how aid will be given and what guarantees will be required of the recipient countries to ensure that the aid is properly used—and these guarantees have been considerably more stringent than those exacted in the major country-to-country programs.

ECOSOC coordinates the work of a complex network of U.N. bodies, semi-autonomous agencies, and the independent agencies related to the U.N. by special agreements. These agencies are called the U.N. family—an apt metaphor to describe both the functioning and the general spirit of these organizations of international cooperation. Sometimes, a certain amount of sibling rivalry exists within the family (just as between departments in the U.S. Federal Government), but all things considered, family members cooperate with a minimum of friction. In itself, this cooperation is remarkable, because several important members of the U.N. family are older than the U.N. itself, and they were originally designed to exercise their functions independently. The whole concept of international cooperation to foster development—rather than merely to regulate technical matters or prevent the spread of epidemics, for instance—is, indeed, recent. That such cooperation has progressed as rapidly as it has in the past twenty years under the aegis of the United Nations is one of the organization's finest, and perhaps most insufficiently appreciated, achievements.

The two oldest members of the U.N. family are the International Telecommunications Union (ITU) and the Universal Postal Union (UPU). The ITU originated in the International Telegraph Union, founded in 1865 to regulate European telegraph and, later, telephone service across national frontiers. The ITU now has 117 members and 2 associate members. It is currently involved in a series of studies on the techniques of using man-made satellites such as Telstar and their effect on international broadcasting frequencies. Among its other vital contributions is the now famous "hot line" between the Kremlin and the White House, made possible only by the preparatory work of the ITU. The UPU, founded in 1874, not only regulates international mail services but acts as a clearing house for settling international postal accounts. Both these agencies were established for practical reasons of self-interest. Even the hypernationalistic governments of the late nineteenth century realized that to keep channels of communication open, some restrictions had to be imposed on the right of a sovereign state to regulate all things according to its own convenience.

Early efforts at international cooperation in the field of health were also rooted in self-interest in a rather narrow sense of the word: the desire of the major temperate-zone powers to keep tropical plagues from spreading to their home territories. The Office International d'Hygiène Publique, established in 1903 by agreement among twelve countries, had grown to include sixty member states by the outbreak of World War I. Its functions were largely restricted to prescribing international quarantine regulations, however.

International cooperation in certain social fields made considerable progress under the League of Nations. The League established a permanent intelligence service to collect and disseminate data on epidemic diseases that might spread from country to country. Its malaria commission concerned itself with how outbreaks of the disease might be controlled as well as with how its spread might be avoided. The League's Covenant specifically entrusted it with "general supervision over agreements with regard . . . to the traffic in opium and other dangerous drugs." By the start of World War II, the League was supervising a world-wide control system designed to limit the manufacture and shipment of narcotic drugs to amounts actually needed for medical and scientific purposes. The

League also supervised international agreements against traffic in women and children, the so-called white-slave trade.

The International Labour Organisation (ILO) was created concurrently with the League of Nations by the Treaty of Versailles. (The United States, which never ratified the Versailles Treaty or joined the League, did become a member of the ILO in 1934.) Its principal mission in the years between World War I and World War II was the formulation of an international labor code designed to protect workers—and particularly women and children—against exploitation and occupational hazards and to assure them certain basic rights. Governments ratifying the various "conventions" making up the labor code pledged themselves to take all measures necessary to carry out the prescribed regulations. Though many governments did not ratify important sections of the code, the ILO's efforts undoubtedly helped eradicate some of the worst labor abuses, such as the use of women in mines, and, by urging on governments a kind of world-wide "bill of rights for labor," hastened the advent of modern labor legislation in many countries.

Another of ILO's valuable activities is in setting up worker-training courses in various countries. The pilot program was launched in Yugoslavia, where it proved to be well adapted to the needs of the country. Former trainees are now employed in a variety of industries. For example, at a leading pulp and paper factory in Prijédor, Bosnia, the production department and all production sections are headed by former ILO trainees, constituting a young, enthusiastic, and evidently very efficient team. Similarly, ILO trainees are reported to be doing an excellent job at the "3 Maj" shipyard in Rieka, which is one of the three most important shipbuilding centers in Yugoslavia.

This worker-training program has grown tremendously over the years. Trainees from Afghanistan, Colombia, Greece, India, Iran, Israel, Jordan, Lebanon, Pakistan, and Turkey, and elsewhere have gone through courses and have been placed in nearly every country in Western Europe, Scandinavia, the U.S.S.R., Czechoslovakia, Australia, Burma, and Tunisia. This partial list underlines the nonpolitical, non-Cold War aspect of the program. The trainees have helped out as foremen and skilled workmen in such industrial complexes as railway workshops, mechanical engineering and automobile manufacturing, iron and steel plants, chemical laboratories, shipyards, oil refineries, hydroelectric installations, textile, paper, leather, and rubber manufacturing, and the woodwork and printing trades.

The closing years of World War II and the early postwar years were the great agency-building period. The first of the new "United Nations" agencies (the term "United Nations," devised by Roosevelt and Churchill, was first used to designate the grand alliance that brought the Axis powers to their knees) was created by conferences of the Allied powers held in 1943 and 1944. The U.N. organization itself did not come into being until the 1945 conference in San Francisco.

The Food and Agriculture Organization of the United Nations (FAO) was established by the Hot Springs Conference of 1943. The World Bank (officially, the International Bank for Reconstruction and Development, or IBRD) and the International Monetary Fund (IMF) were created by the Bretton Woods Conference of 1944.

All three new agencies were created in anticipation of postwar problems of reconstruction and development. Of the three, the IMF exemplifies best the international agency as an indispensable regulatory body. The need for such an agency was clearly apparent by the early 1940's. The preceding decade had been an era of international monetary chaos. Following the widespread abandonment of the gold standard, sudden currency devaluations and wildly fluctuating exchange rates had compounded the difficulties of world recovery from the Great Depression. Since the European powers were emerging from World War II with their gold and dollar reserves practically exhausted, there was talk of creating a kind of international Federal Reserve Bank to restore international credit. As finally agreed upon, the IMF was considerably less than that, but with reserves of convertible currencies and gold originally totaling $8 billion and subsequently increased to $15 billion, the Fund was able to maintain international balance-of-payments liquidity throughout the period of postwar reconstruction without major currency dislocations, at least so far as Western Europe was concerned. IMF transactions are extremely complicated and technical, but in general terms, the Fund's reserves come from paid-in subscriptions by member states. They serve as a kind of monetary flywheel; members can draw on the Fund's resources against their own currencies, but only to meet temporary balance-of-payments difficulties. IMF resources are not, however, available for investment and, except as they promote monetary stability, play no part in the development programs being pursued by the other members of the U.N. family.

The FAO and the World Bank, on the other hand, were conceived of quite differently—not as regulatory agencies, but as development agencies, and, as such, they set the tone for the later additions to the U.N. economic and social system. The preamble to the FAO constitution pledges member states to promote the common welfare through separate and collective action to raise levels of nutrition and standards of living, to improve the production and distribution of all food and agricultural products, to better the conditions of rural populations, and thus to contribute toward an expanding world economy. The constitution itself empowers the FAO "to furnish such technical assistance as governments may request," thus foreshadowing a form of aid and cooperation that has become a major feature of the U.N. system.

The World Bank, in certain respects, operates much like any investment bank. It has shareholders—member governments, in this instance—who subscribe varying amounts of capital stock to the Bank. It borrows money by selling World Bank bonds (guaranteed by the member governments) on the international market. It lends money only to enterprises it considers sound risks, and with the additional proviso that the Bank's loan be guaranteed by the government of the country in which the money is to be used. Here the similarity to an ordinary bank ends. The World Bank is primarily concerned, not with the profitability to itself of its investments, but of their profitability to the countries where they are placed. The $5 billion in loans that the Bank has placed in Africa, Asia, Europe, and Latin America has been used to forge the sinews of awakening economies. Prominent among the projects the Bank has supported have been irrigation and power generation; roads, ports, and communication networks; mines; natural-gas pipelines; and steel mills. Industries and services like these are sometimes spoken of as the "economic infrastructure" of a country; this means they are the foundation blocks, the underpinnings that must be laid before further industrial development can take place. The World Bank does not compete with private investment. It enters the picture only in situations in which private investment is not available or is not available in sufficient amounts. And on many occasions, World Bank investments have paved the way for significant investments in the private sector—for cheap power, good transportation, and good communications attract industry.

The San Francisco Conference, which met in June, 1945, to draft the U.N. Charter, agreed that one of the objectives of the U.N. should be to promote international cultural and educational cooperation, but the consensus was that a separate organization was required for that purpose. Accordingly, a conference was convened in London, in November of that year, at which a new agency was organized—the United Nations Educational, Scientific and Cultural Organization, better known by its acronym, UNESCO. The preamble to the

UNESCO constitution opens with the words: "Since wars begin in the minds of men, it is in the minds of men that the defenses of peace must be constructed." With a membership even broader than the U.N.'s—West Germany, South Korea, South Vietnam, Switzerland, and Monaco, none of which are U.N. members, belong not only to UNESCO but to a number of the other agencies—UNESCO has sponsored numerous projects for the dissemination of knowledge for better understanding in "the minds of men" of different countries.

However, although UNESCO is one of the most active, it is at the same time one of the most criticized, of the Specialized Agencies of the United Nations. I would like, therefore, to discuss the criticism at the outset, because this agency has been singled out so often that through sheer repetition the propaganda attacking it may have come to be believed. Merely to deny dozens of assorted charges of ultraliberalism, socialism, and even Communism would not be particularly helpful, but it may be of some use to explore the organization and realize what makes it tick.

In the first place, people who are deeply interested in raising the standard of literacy around the world, interested in bringing world cultures together for study and development, interested in the application of research in scientific areas on world-wide problems—all these are bound to be international-minded people.

In the second place, the latest programs of the agency throw into bold relief the principle under which it has always operated: namely, that to expose people to only one ideology or "ism" or type of culture is one of the worst services you can do them. Those who are ready to believe and to repeat stories about Communist influence in the agency should be given the opportunity of hearing UNESCO people talk about the horrors of intellectual bondage under the restrictive practices applied against Communist authors, musicians, poets, and the like. They should hear the open statements attacking the whole Iron Curtain concept as applied to public education and public opinion. Thus we find that one of the two major projects mentioned in the official description of the agency is "for appreciation of Eastern and Western cultural values." This does not mean that Westerners alone are to be exposed to Eastern cultures, nor does the word "Eastern" carry any Cold War implication. They consider this a two-way street between the different cultures of the world, and naturally classify Japan, the Philippines, Thailand, and other friends of the U.S. as "Eastern," which of course they are.

Thus UNESCO has a sense of value that should shock only those who will not believe in the free and broad dissemination of intellectual material, lest some of it might influence the thinking of people. Those who dread comparison of Communist ideas with those of the free world, and fear contacts on the intellectual level among educators, artists, scientists, musicians, and authors regardless of country of origin, will continue to suspect the worst. In my opinion, the readiness of this agency to help in the exposure of ideas on a mutual basis is of great assistance to our own ideology. If the contrary were true, then our ideology must be badly presented and "sold."

Finally, when we look squarely at the official records of the organization, we find that although it became a member of the United Nations family in December of 1946, the Soviet Union did not become a member of the agency until late 1954, and no Soviet national occupied an important official capacity until 1961, when a Soviet was appointed one of the deputy directors. From the record, and from my experience, I think it is obvious that there has been no untoward Soviet or other Communist influence in the short but praiseworthy history of this organization.

As to specific examples of its work, the following may be considered almost routine. In Morocco, the government decided to extend a literacy campaign that a UNESCO expert had successfully started in one limited pilot area. In this case, the expert drew on his knowledge of Arabic culture and rural customs in North Africa to institute a daily practice of town meetings, at which literacy lessons were given by the village elders. To do this, they were first given training through radios that were distributed by the government. Some 1,200 receivers were distributed for the purpose and approximately 200,000 people learned to use a basic written vocabulary that had been prepared by the expert himself.

A project in Mexico involves the improvement of higher technical education in relation to the industrial development needs of the country, and has been jointly conducted, since 1958, by the Ministry of Education and the Bank of Mexico, which have been assisting the universities and technological institutes of the Mexican states. New laboratories have been aided, and curriculums have been modernized in industrial chemistry, biology, physics, electronics, chemical engineering, and other subjects. More than 100 former fellows have returned to these institutes, mostly graduates of UNESCO Fellowship Programs.

In Madagascar, a rural-education project is adapting primary instruction for economic and social development. One expert is working to establish the organization and programs for an initial four-year course, which would educate more than 71 per cent of the school-age population in ten years. He is also working on an accelerated program to train teachers for rural schools. A second expert is preparing textual material. A third is organizing a pilot traveling library. This plan is included in the general program of scholastic development, which in turn is part of the national plan for economic and social development. Moreover, a primary-education system will be established in certain schools that are more closely associated with the life of rural communities and that will harmonize with other projects of regional development, such as cooperative education and education for nutrition.

The high cost of school buildings is a serious obstacle to the extension of education in the Sudan. Accordingly, an expert, combining the functions of an architect and a civil engineer, was assigned to develop an inexpensive school-building program using locally available material. After visiting different parts of the country to study the existing schools, he prepared designs for primary-, intermediate-, and secondary-level schools of various sizes to suit different geographical areas. In addition, the expert carried out research into the use of locally available materials—cement monoblocks, roofing slabs (using local grasses and cement), water repellents, and bamboo walls —and submitted these to various tests to determine their strength and durability until he came up with a cheap and long-lasting combination.

Many problems, both geographical and sociological, had to be resolved in carrying out the project of the Women's Education Center in the Fezzan in Libya. The school had to be established as a boarding school because of the lack of transportation facilities; the fact that young girls and women are not normally allowed to go away from home was an additional difficulty to be overcome.

Thanks to the tact shown by the UNESCO expert and the confidence he inspired, parents have allowed their daughters of intermediate-school age to board away from home and to be trained as future teachers. Two classes have been recruited and courses are conducted in academic subjects (arithmetic, history, and Arabic) and in subjects suitable for adult education (mother and child care, hygiene, gardening, nutrition, and sewing). Both courses have been considered necessary since the girl trainees will later be called upon to teach adults as well as schoolchildren.

A Regional Center for Reading Material Production in South Asia was initiated in 1955. This project covered a wide range of objectives—to stimulate and improve book-production and book-distribution techniques, to strengthen the existing agencies, to create national book trusts, to train personnel by providing expert services and fellowships, to organize seminars, workshops, and training courses, and to give encouragement to authors and publishers.

To start with, four countries participated in the project—Burma, Ceylon, India, and Pakistan; but since January, 1959, Iran has also participated. Originally confined to "new literates," the project has been widened in scope to embrace "new readers," those who already possess some reading ability.

Assistance has been provided to accredited agencies for the preparation and production of a series of model books on international understanding and simple science in the main languages of the project area—Burmese, Singhalese, Hindi, Urdu, Bengali, and Tamil. Some 150 titles have been produced so far; and 500 copies of each published book have been distributed free to libraries, reading rooms, and institutions.

In these days of precarious relations all over the world, which can often be traced to poor communications between governments and peoples, any organization that so perseveringly furthers the cause of literacy and understanding between human beings must be counted on the side of the angels.

Thus, by February, 1946, when the Economic and Social Council met for its first session, a good beginning for the U.N. family of agencies had been made. The UPU, the ITU, and the ILO were long-established agencies, about to be incorporated into the U.N. family through special agreements. The FAO, the World Bank, and the International Monetary Fund had already begun work, and UNESCO was to start within the year.

One of ECOSOC's first actions was to call for a conference to establish a full-fledged international health agency. At a meeting held in New York in the summer of 1946, the constitution of the World Health Organization (WHO) was drawn up. The birth of the organization was delayed until April, 1948, however, by the failure of some governments to act quickly on ratification, and an interim commission was formed to carry on such vital quarantine and epidemiological functions as it could. One of the crises with which the interim commission had to deal was the 1947–48 cholera epidemic in Egypt, affecting areas on both sides of the Suez Canal. The cholera panic, more than any other single event, demonstrated the need for an international health agency, and as the epidemic raged, the ratifications of the WHO constitution, which were to clinch the organization's existence, started pouring in. Before the epidemic was stamped out, it had claimed more than 20,000 lives, but the prompt action of the WHO interim commission at least prevented the spread of the epidemic beyond Egyptian territory. "It was," WHO later reported, "as if a major war had been averted."

Of all the United Nations family, including the U.N. itself, WHO has come to have the widest membership and is the closest to a "universal agency." It is as apolitical as its enemies —the bacteria, viruses, and insect carriers of malaria, yellow fever, and sleeping sickness, which do not acknowledge the existence of national frontiers. WHO enlists the aid of every country on earth, with the exception of mainland China and the Communist sectors of the countries partitioned in the Cold War—North Korea, North Vietnam, and East Germany—in the exchange of information vital to the war against disease. It was the only agency whose representatives were allowed to remain in Indonesia when that country withdrew from the U.N. on March 1, 1965. In the matter of international cooperation, I am afraid that the medical men of the world have put the rest of us to shame.

WHO has gone far beyond the old idea that the primary function of an international health agency is to police a *cordon sanitaire* between plague-ridden and salubrious climes. With the advances in medical science that have taken place in the past thirty years, most of the diseases that make India, for instance, a more dangerous place in which to live than the

United States could be wiped out if decent health services could be organized and if rudimentary principles of hygiene and nutrition could be popularized. WHO's philosophy is that the best way of checking the spread of disease is to root it out at its point of origin. WHO advisers are at work in more than a hundred countries, helping governments to develop permanent health services and apply the latest findings of medical science to the control of such diseases as malaria, yaws, and tuberculosis. Now inoculation and vaccination needles are known and welcomed in parts of the world that a decade ago knew only the rites of tribal medicine men.

Before the agency-spawning movement that accompanied the end of World War II had exhausted itself, five other independent intergovernmental organizations joined the U.N. family. These were the International Civil Aeronautics Organization (ICAO); the World Meteorological Organization (WMO); the Inter-Governmental Maritime Consultative Organization (IMCO); the International Atomic Energy Agency (IAEA); and two affiliates of the World Bank, the International Finance Corporation (IFC) and the International Development Association (IDA).

Without disparaging their importance in any way, I shall discuss the civil aeronautics, meteorological, and maritime organizations only briefly. Their functions are basically technical, regulatory, or legal, and, like the ITU and the UPU, they *had* to exist sooner or later if international intercourse were not to become hopelessly bogged down.

Governments have to agree on certain procedures covering international flights, or there can be no regularly scheduled international flight services (and in a day and age when, at short notice, heads of state are accustomed to visiting countries on the opposite side of the earth to pursue their political aims, the failure of these services would be unthinkable. The ICAO, among other things, codifies international air law, promotes the standardization of technical equipment, coordinates such joint navigational services as the nine floating ocean stations in the North Atlantic, and works to reduce customs and immigration red tape at international airports. It also lends aid on domestic projects, such as one recently undertaken in Peru. This ICAO project now owns six aircraft for flight instruction, one Link trainer, spare parts, classroom equipment, and all necessary technical textbooks. Runway facilities have been improved and maintenance workshops completed. Personnel have been recruited, including mechanics, flight instructors, control-tower operators, clerks, and manual workers. It is expected that Peru will soon have qualified commercial pilots and aircraft mechanics, who are badly needed in a country where frequently the only means of transport is by air. Related projects will be undertaken soon, including landing strips at strategic points throughout the country.

According to all experts in the field, the ICAO has been a prime factor in building our own billion-dollar private-enterprise aircraft industry, and has helped all other members to a commensurate degree. World safety standards promulgated by the ICAO have made possible low insurance rates, which in turn have enabled banks, insurance companies, and governments to lay out billions to buyers and manufacturers of aircraft.

In all these varied aspects, international cooperation in the field of civil aviation, like international cooperation in the field of postal services, works so smoothly today that we hardly notice its existence—but we would notice it very quickly indeed if it broke down.

The World Meteorological Organization is the indispensable liaison agency that has enabled governments on both sides of the Iron Curtain and on all continents to weld their far-flung meteorological services into something very close to a global network. One of the organization's most important, and deceptively routine, functions is the gathering of comprehensive and up-to-the-minute weather information. Every day, more than 8,000 ground stations, 3,000 aircraft, and 3,000 ships transmit 100,000 weather observations from the surface of the earth and 10,000 more from the upper atmosphere. In this function, we see how the scope of the WMO, like that of many other agencies, has been violently expanded by recent technological advances. The land stations and weather ships were formerly deemed adequate to the job, but manned weather-observation aircraft flights are beginning to supplement them, and the U.S. development of the Tiros-type weather satellite in orbit around the world carries meteorological observation still further. Although the United States has taken the lead in developing this technology, nearly all information gathered by the satellite system will be shared with the rest of the world.

Another example of the way WMO works is a project started in 1956 to establish the relationship between locust swarms and the meteorological factors obtaining in areas regularly devastated by this plague—the arid zones of Africa and the Middle East. These swarms can descend in an area with lightning speed and destroy an entire crop within a very short time. Crop damage caused by locusts has run to as much as $30,000,000 annually.

To control these swarms, it was essential to establish the exact relations between breeding and movement of locust swarms on the one hand and the corresponding meteorological factors on the other. But this was not possible in the absence of comprehensive meteorological maps for the infested regions. Accordingly, a technical mission consisting of two WMO experts was set up to collect all available meteorological information from Africa, the Mediterranean, and the Middle East for one test year chosen for the study.

This important project has received sizable assistance from the U.N.'s Expanded Program of Technical Assistance and other sources—approximately $1,100,000, exclusive of the substantial counterpart expenditures incurred by the High

Commission for British East Africa. The experience gained in this project will be of great value to the larger desert locust control project, to which the Special Fund has allocated $2,800,000. In addition, for the first time, complete meteorological maps are available for a large area on both sides of the equator. They will help improve weather forecasting in the tropics, which in turn will benefit aviation, navigation, and agriculture.

A completely different sort of project, but one of equal or even greater value for the future, involved the water resources of Latin America. Following a resolution adopted by the Economic Commission for Latin America, a team was established in 1957 to carry out a preliminary study of the water resources and the prospects of their future use. The WMO obtained the services of a hydrometeorological expert to join the ECLA team, which completed surveys of water resources in Chile, North Patagonia, and Ecuador; and in October, 1959, it proceeded to Venezuela to commence its survey there. The studies and appraisals of new and existing data made by the WMO expert on the team showed concretely that the present meteorological and hydrological observation networks are insufficient for obtaining the necessary data for agricultural development, hydroelectric schemes, and other purposes, including civil aviation.

Partly as a result of these findings, two countries in Latin America—Chile and Ecuador—developed projects for extending and completing their meteorological and hydrological networks as part of their programs for economic development, and they requested assistance from the Special Fund. In response to these requests, the governing council of the Fund, at its December, 1959, session, approved a contribution of $612,500 to Chile and $405,500 to Ecuador. The WMO was requested to act as the executing agency for these two projects. In this intricate dovetailing of resources and skills among U.N. agencies, we see again how cooperation on an international scale has grown beyond the initial fact-gathering process, although that remains an essential prerequisite.

The Inter-Governmental Maritime Consultative Organization, not formally established until 1959, is the youngest of these agencies. Its job is to promote cooperation and exchange of information on technical matters affecting ocean shipping. It is also concerned with safety at sea and improved navigation. Standards developed by the Organization and adopted by its members have resulted in the saving of many lives and millions of dollars' worth of cargo.

The International Atomic Energy Agency is in a category by itself, and for a very good reason. It deals with a two-edged sword—the ultimate in two-edged swords, one might say. Atomic energy is capable, on the one hand, of providing man with a limitless source of power for desalting oceans, exploring space, or any other enterprise he has a mind to undertake. It is also capable, on the other hand, of extinguishing the human race in the twinkling of an eye.

The idea for an "Atoms for Peace" agency was broached to the General Assembly in 1953 by President Eisenhower. The President said that he hoped the atomic powers, through such an agency, would dedicate "some of their strength to serve the needs rather than the fears of mankind." As Chief of the U.S. Delegation, I had the honor of participating in the difficult and delicate negotiations among the atomic powers— and between the atomic powers and the atomic "have-not" powers—that brought the IAEA into being in the summer of 1957. It occupies a somewhat privileged position in the U.N. family, reporting to the General Assembly rather than to ECOSOC and, if need be, directly to the Security Council itself.

Georgi Zaroubin, Soviet Ambassador to the United States from 1952 to 1958, was in charge of the Soviet Delegation all through the 1956 negotiations on the statute or charter of the IAEA. Big and burly, he was a most forceful individual, and at the same time a very gracious and well-intentioned human being. Not once in all the give and take of private and public effort that attended this long-drawn-out negotiation did he ever resort to vilification or propagandistic oratory. Even more important, he was meticulous in fulfilling his commitments and promises. Never once did he go back on his word, and I responded in kind.

The only time he showed displeasure with me was once when specific instructions to oppose one of his suggestions reached me too late to notify him of what seemed to be a change of position on our part. He quickly received confirmation of my statement that I had tried in vain to reach him before that particular session of the meeting, and "forgave" me my trespasses in most earthy terms. Zaroubin's insistence on the letter of agreements between us was so strong that at one point he made a speech in the eighty-two-nation ratifying session in opposition to an amendment put forward by two East European-bloc countries. When I expressed appreciation afterward, he merely snorted: "I promised you we would hold the line, didn't I?"

IAEA is charged with assisting the widest possible application of atomic energy for peaceful purposes while, at the same time, doing everything in its power to discourage the proliferation of nuclear weapons. Since the basic technology is the same in either case, IAEA's mission is not a simple one. Its activities include: providing assistance in atomic research, development, and applications; arranging exchanges of information and specialists; and making provision for the training of personnel in various member countries having appropriate facilities. The Agency also operates a reactor training school in Vienna, its headquarters, with equipment donated by the United States. It supplies or arranges for the supply of materials, equipment, and facilities for approved projects, establishes safety standards and procedures, and furnishes technical assistance to its eighty-seven members.

The Agency has developed elaborate safeguards to ensure that no nuclear materials that pass through its hands or that are produced with its assistance are diverted to military ends. The vote on inspection for these safeguards, in 1963, marked the first time in history that the Soviet Union supported *with a vote* the principle of on-site inspection. Due to the generosity of the United States, an ample supply of material for building and using reactors is available, and the construction of facilities with equipment is proceeding apace. The Agency has not realized its full potential by any means, but it is hoped that the safeguards adopted in 1963 will prove the breakthrough point. It is conceivable that if the nuclear powers ever negotiate a meaningful treaty to prevent the spread of nuclear weapons, the IAEA will be the agency chosen to police it.

The two affiliates of the World Bank were established to broaden the Bank's work. The International Finance Corporation, established in 1956, owes its existence to the belief that there is no substitute for efficiently managed private enterprise in economic development. (The Soviet bloc would disagree, of course; but since the U.S.S.R. never took advantage of its right to become a charter member of the Bank, the Bank and its affiliates have not been obliged to trim their sails to Communist economic theories.) The IFC invests in new or expanding industrial enterprises in conjunction with private capital. It carries on its business in the same way as a private underwriter, carefully investigating the profit potentials of the enterprises it backs, but unlike the Bank itself, the IFC requires no government guarantees for its underwritings.

Starting with initial capital of $100 million (subscribed by member governments), the IFC has consistently realized a reasonable profit on its investments. These profits have covered the agency's operating expenses of about $2.5 million a year and have enabled it gradually to build up its capital. By the end of 1964, gross IFC investments had totaled $128 million, mostly in manufacturing and processing industries, such as fertilizers, textiles, building materials, lumber and mill products, and petrochemicals. The IFC has been particularly active in Latin America, where private enterprise has traditionally assumed a primary role in development.

The International Development Association was established in 1960 to meet an urgent need of another kind: financing for projects that could not be considered class-A bank risks but that nevertheless were vital to future economic growth. There is an old saying that a banker will not lend you money unless you can prove you don't need it. The World Bank never lent money unless the need could be clearly established, but because of the strict credit and repayment conditions that circumscribed its operations, the Bank found great difficulty in helping many of the countries that most needed international assistance. The IDA, with a "soft loan" policy as opposed to the Bank's "hard loan" approach, was created to channel a greater proportion of U.N. development loans to countries unable to meet the Bank's terms.

With an initial capitalization of $1 billion (subscribed by sixty-eight members), the IDA commenced operations with large loans for highway improvement, port development, agricultural irrigation, and urban water supplies. By the end of 1964, total credits extended had come to slightly more than the agency's initial capitalization. Negotiations were under way with member governments to increase their subscriptions, and an arrangement was being worked out to channel some of the Bank's earnings (more than half a billion dollars over the years) into the IDA. IDA credits are generally extended for a period of fifty years at no interest—though there is a small service charge—with repayment commencing after ten years. Under its Articles of Agreement, the IDA is authorized to support any project that "will make an important contribution to the development of the area or areas concerned, whether or not the project is revenue producing and directly productive." Though a young agency, the IDA has already built up a record to be proud of, and like its parent body, the World Bank, has impressed observers everywhere with its efficient use of the assistance funds at its disposal. (Among those it has most impressed is Senator J. W. Fulbright, Chairman of the Senate Committee on Foreign Relations, who has repeatedly urged the United States Government to channel a greater share of its foreign aid through the IDA and the other U.N. agencies. As Senator Fulbright recently told the committee: "I have never seen a sign that said 'World Bank, Go Home.' ")

The fourteen agencies I have just discussed are the independent members of the U.N. family—the adults sitting in at the family conferences, so to speak. As it has been built up over the years, this system includes ten technical agencies, specializing respectively in postal services; communications; labor; food and agriculture; health; education, science, and culture; air transport; meteorology; atomic energy; and maritime affairs. The system also includes four banking agencies, whose functions range from currency stabilization to development loans. Each agency has its own membership, its own headquarters, its own budget, and its own administrative staff. Though all maintain permanent representatives at the Glass House, none of them actually works out of New York. Indeed, the "family" is fairly well scattered over the principal cities of Europe and North America. The four banking agencies—the IMF, the World Bank, the IFC, and the IDA—have their headquarters in Washington, D.C. Geneva, where excellent conference facilities were developed in the days of the League of Nations, is the headquarters city for four of the technical agencies—the ILO, WHO, the ITU, and the WMO. The other headquarters are scattered: the UPU in Bern, the FAO in Rome, UNESCO in Paris, the IAEA in Vienna, the ICAO in Montreal, and the IMCO in London.

Considering their world-wide responsibilities, the agencies operate on very modest budgets. WHO has the largest budget,

$38,360,000 for 1965; followed by UNESCO, with $48,-857,000 for the two years 1965 and 1966. The FAO, which also handles its accounts on a two-year basis, had a $38,000,000 budget for 1964 and 1965; and the ILO had an $18,684,000 budget for 1965. These are the "big four" among the technical agencies in terms of direct assistance to the developing countries. Besides carrying out considerable research and serving as clearing houses for the exchange of international information, they recruit thousands of international experts, all of them authorities in their fields, to help the developing countries fight disease, increase food production, and strengthen their schools and training institutions. The other technical agencies, which are not so heavily involved in direct assistance activities, operate on considerably smaller budgets, ranging from a little over $1 million a year for the UPU to about $8 million for the IAEA. All told, the budgets of the ten technical agencies total about $120 million a year. This money is raised by assessments against the member countries of the various agencies, levied roughly in proportion to their national income. The administrative expenses of the four banking agencies (about $40 million per year) are paid from their earnings.

Before ending this description of the autonomous agencies of the U.N., I would like to point out that one much-needed agency has still not yet achieved full status: the International Trade Organization (ITO); and trade, of course, is the life-blood of development. A United Nations conference in Havana in 1947–48 drew up a charter for an ITO, but it is still operating as a temporary organization. The reason for this is simple: The Charter provided that, in order to come into force, the United States had to ratify it, along with the other major powers. When the matter came before the United States Congress, however, certain powerful protectionist interests and several leading Senators launched such a bitter attack upon it that it could not be approved for ratification.

It was therefore decided, rather than let the whole area

of trade go by the board, to form a General Agreement on Tariffs and Trade. Since this did not need a treaty charter, it would not have to be ratified. Even though GATT consists of only forty-four members and eight other affiliates, it does represent some 85 per cent of all world trade and, as a result, controls these matters to a large degree.

There are few more important functions in the whole United Nations than those of GATT. One need only read accounts of the sessions of GATT and of the desperately hard bargaining that goes on at them to realize that the economic lifeblood of most of these nations is in constant danger from the hyper-nationalist high tariff walls which are so often demanded by the various interests of many of the others. It is a constant struggle, only a bit less deadly than the politico-military threats raised by the Cold War. The developing countries have especially found themselves in an increasingly serious trade bind in the past decade. Whereas the prices of the primary commodities they export have remained almost static, the prices of the manufactured goods they import have risen by a good 10 per cent. The developing countries have been pushing vigorously for some kind of dynamic trade agency to promote long-term solutions to this problem. No agency has yet been formed, but a United Nations Conference on Trade and Development was held in Geneva in 1964 and is scheduled to meet every three years. Furthermore, as part of the U.N. itself, a fifty-five nation Trade and Development Board has been organized, which will meet regularly in the Glass House. Meanwhile, the autonomous trade organization that was envisaged almost twenty years ago as a vital part of the U.N. system remains the conspicuous "specter at the feast" of the Specialized Agencies.

If the autonomous agencies can be regarded as members of the U.N. "extended family," there is an equally important group of economic and social bodies that can be said to belong to the U.N. "inner family." In the technical language em-

ployed in the Glass House, they are "organs" of the United
Nations—its eyes, ears, hands, and feet, so to speak, in the war
against the causes of war.

The U.N. bodies designed to eliminate unnecessary causes
of friction in international affairs and to stamp out social
abuses derive in principle directly from the League of Nations
system. The International Law Commission, established by the
General Assembly in 1947 to encourage the codification and
progressive development of international law, deals, of course,
with a subject antedating the League by centuries; other
bodies, such as the Committee on the Peaceful Uses of Outer
Space, deal with concerns of more recent origin. This Committee, formed in 1959 at the instigation of the United States, is
working on, among other things, agreements concerning lia-
bility for damage caused by objects launched into outer space
and on agreements regarding assistance to astronauts and space
vehicles, similar to those now in force for assistance to ships
at sea. Although this Committee must be classed as one designed to eradicate national frictions, it has encountered its
share of friction, largely because the U.S.S.R. and the U.S.
have been unable to agree on certain political matters involving the nationality of conference staffs. But, at the same time,
as a collateral result of the Committee's existence, we should
note that the United States and the Union of Soviet Socialist
Republics jointly sponsored a resolution in the Eighteenth
General Assembly banning the orbiting of any nuclear device
or weapon. This may presage a clearer road not only for the
Committee but for the whole United Nations family, although
we are told that certain members of the Committee have expressed annoyance that the two outer-space powers apparently
came to this agreement without reference to the other members of the group. Another example of the old saying: "You
can't win!"

Outer space is not the only thorny region the U.N. has
tackled via the committee or commission approach. The

Commission on the Status of Women has spearheaded world-wide efforts to guarantee women their full and equal "civil rights." The U.N.'s Commission on Narcotic Drugs assists and advises the Economic and Social Council in the regulatory functions that the latter inherited from the League. I developed a healthy admiration for the scope of the Commission's activities during the few days I sat in on it as a substitute for Harry Anslinger, long our regular representative and now retired. Its work in narcotics control is not limited to supervising the various international treaties on traffic in narcotics, but goes far beyond into conducting studies on drug addiction, maintaining a laboratory for determining the geographical origin of opiates seized in international traffic, and in cooperation with WHO, keeping under constant review any new and possibly addictive substances, such as barbiturates, amphetamines, and tranquilizers.

Because there is no autonomous "social welfare" agency at the international level, one of the departments of the U.N. Secretariat, the United Nations Bureau of Social Affairs, working under the direction of the Social Commission, has come to exercise certain agency functions concerning what might be termed "the human aspects of development." The Bureau conducts studies and surveys in such areas as housing, urbanization, welfare, and the social consequences of the sweeping economic changes now taking place over most of the globe. It also works with the governments of developing countries in an advisory capacity to strengthen their social services and to deal with such growing problems as slums and juvenile delinquency.

No human problem has been better publicized in our era than the tragic plight of political refugees. Most governments can find excuses for looking the other way once they have gotten their political advantages out of a situation, but the United Nations cannot. (Governments have a tendency to dump particularly intransigent problems in the U.N.'s "lap," and when great power rivalries do not preclude a solution, the U.N. usually gives a good accounting of itself.) I have already discussed the United Nations Relief and Works Agency for Palestine Refugees (UNRWA), which, since 1949, has been providing food, shelter, education, and vocational training for Arab refugees. But there are sizable numbers of refugees from other quarters—refugees from Communist China who have sought asylum in Hong Kong; refugees from tribal warfare in Central Africa; a handful, still in special camps in Europe, who are refugees from World War II. A United Nations High Commissioner for Refugees is charged with the nonpolitical and humanitarian task of providing international protection for refugees and promoting permanent solutions to their problems. The present High Commissioner is Prince Sadruddin Aga Khan, an Iranian national, who in January, 1966, succeeded Felix Schnyder of Switzerland. (Although Switzerland has never joined the U.N. proper, it has cooperated wholeheartedly in the economic and social activities of the U.N. family.) The High Commissioner's Office played a key role in resettling the European refugees from World War II and from the Hungarian Revolution of 1956. It extended its protection to refugees from the Algerian War who fled to Morocco and Tunisia. More recently, the Commissioner's Office has lent its assistance to the government of Hong Kong in helping the million Chinese refugees who have sought asylum there. It has also lent its good offices to help the various refugees who have sought asylum across international borders in Central Africa.

People frequently ask me: "What is the U.N. doing about the population problem?" The answer is that the U.N. has done more than any other organization in the world to call attention to the population problem and to encourage nations to think in terms of a "population policy" for the future. The so-called population explosion is, indeed, one of the most serious problems of our time. In most of the developing nations, hungry to begin with, population is increasing just as fast as agricultural production; in a considerable number of them, it is increasing faster. A study of population trends shows that we can expect the world's present population of about 3.2 billion to rise to 6 billion or perhaps 7 billion by the end of this century. This is going to make the task of raising living standards in the developing countries, where most of the population increase will take place, almost impossibly difficult. Since its creation in 1946, the U.N.'s Population Commission has issued a number of solemn warnings on this subject. Indeed, the fact that the population problem is so widely appreciated today must be largely credited to the work of the Commission. The U.N. has sponsored a number of studies, meetings, and seminars on population problems. For its part, WHO has been reviewing the biological factors affecting human fertility. So far, the U.N. has not been able to proceed beyond the stage of investigating population problems and keeping a close watch on population trends. A proposal to allow the organization to provide technical assistance to governments, on their request, in the field of family planning was voted down by the General Assembly in 1963. The position of the Economic and Social Council is that it is up to every government to work out and implement such family-planning policies as it sees fit. Readers who think the U.N. should be doing *more*, in a concrete way, about the population problem should urge their governments to take such a stand in the General Assembly.

The "inner family" activities I have so far described— including those concerned with outer space—fall within the traditional jurisdiction of international bodies as conceived prior to World War II: law, regulation, the harmonization of national interests. Even the work of the Population Commission derives from the League's efforts to obtain comparable census statistics from the various countries of the world and to find out "how many of us there are and how fast we are multiplying."

In response to the demands of the post-World War II era, the United Nations shifted its attention from protection and information-gathering to a wholly new field—development. As a result, the inner family now includes an entire dynamic component of "commissions," "funds," and other organs specifically concerned with development; this concept has been defined by the United Nations as "growth plus change."

A majority of the present members of the U.N. were colonies when the organization was first established. Their preoccupation in the debates of the Economic and Social Council and the General Assembly has been: "What do we do to catch up with the rest of the world?" The effect this has had on the international organization itself is well described in a passage from the Secretary General's *Five Year Perspective*, published in 1960:

> The most clearly marked trend in the work of the United Nations organizations in the economic, social and human rights fields is the shift in emphasis to development. . . . There was a primary concern in the League of Nations and the early ILO with action of a defensive or protective nature—the protection of countries against diseases that might cross international frontiers; prevention of international traffic in women and children and in illicit drugs; protection of workers against unfair and inhumane conditions of labor. . . . Such early action in the economic and social field was taken in a climate of thought that hardly recognized the concept of economic development.
>
> Towards the middle of this century, however, the idea of development as a major objective of international cooperation took root in the international scene, and the major goal of the United Nations and the specialized agencies in the economic and social field came to be that of promoting the development of the less developed countries. This purpose was present in the Charter of the United Nations and the constitution of most

of the specialized agencies, but it has undergone a great expansion in practice.

With the shift of emphasis to development, more and more of the energies of the United Nations family have gone into direct assistance to countries through field surveys, advisory services of experts, demonstration and pilot projects, and certain forms of material assistance. In turn, this shift has brought about certain significant changes at headquarters in the actual meaning, or image, of headquarters to its staff. Headquarters is now considered primarily an administrative center, subordinate in significance to much larger and more complex field activities. It is perhaps notable that those winter suntans in the Secretariat Building of the Glass House come not from vacations in Miami, but from field trips to tropical countries, and that one of the memories attendant on these trips is the required preliminary visit to the U.N.'s health center on the fifth floor, for cholera, tetanus, typhoid, and yellow-fever shots.

There are four U.N. regional economic commissions, which serve as decentralized headquarters for planning and development. Each is a kind of miniature U.N. in itself. Three of these "regional economic parliaments" were established early in the history of the U.N. The Economic Commission for Europe (ECE) and the Economic Commission for Asia and the Far East (ECAFE) were established in 1947. The Economic Commission for Latin America (ECLA) was established in 1948. ECE headquarters are in Geneva and ECLA's are in Santiago de Chile. ECAFE headquarters, located in Shanghai before the Communist takeover in China, are now in Bangkok. The youngest, the Economic Commission for Africa (ECA), with headquarters in Addis Ababa, was established in 1958.

Each regional commission serves as a forum where governments consult with one another, exchange information and experience, and endeavor to find ways of solving their com-

mon economic problems. The secretariats of the regional organizations serve as economic intelligence centers, collecting
and publishing a variety of vital information and carrying out
regional and country studies. The regional commissions have
also been responsible for getting a number of practical projects
under way. One of the most ambitious international projects
ever conceived, the Lower Mekong River Project, was
launched by ECAFE. The Mekong rises in Tibet and empties
into the sea south of Saigon, in Vietnam. Its lower basin drains
an area of 235,135 square miles in Cambodia, Laos, Thailand,
and Vietnam. The project is conceived as a kind of a gigantic
TVA to harness the river and its tributaries for power, irrigation, and navigation. Investigations and surveys were started
more than ten years ago, and construction has now begun on
the first dams. The steady progress of the project has been
nothing short of miraculous, in view of the political differences
between some of the countries involved. Thailand and Cambodia have on several occasions virtually severed diplomatic
relations; yet their representatives have continued to confer
amicably on the Mekong project. Even the Communist rebels
in Laos have carefully avoided interfering with preconstruc-
tion surveys in the territory they control.

These regional commissions are generally well thought of;
in each case, they consist of people familiar with and sympathetic to the problems of the area; they epitomize the "do-it-
yourself" concept that is dear to the hearts of all emerging
people as well as of the more developed economies.

Rounding out the U.N. "inner family" and spearheading its
project assistance to the developing countries are the United
Nations Children's Fund, the U.N.'s Technical Assistance
Program, and its Special Fund. (In January, 1966, the latter
two organs were merged into an over-all United Nations
Development Program.) These (along with the World Bank
and its affiliates) provide most of the actual muscle behind the
work the U.N. family is doing to promote economic develop-

ment and improve living conditions in the world's poorer regions. All told, they now provide better than $170 million a year in the kind of aid required to get important new projects off the ground—expert services, supplies, equipment, and stipends for the training of local personnel.

The United Nations Children's Fund, better known as UNICEF, was established by the General Assembly in 1946 to provide emergency assistance to the children of war-devastated countries. In its first three years, UNICEF chalked up a remarkable record, shipping many thousands of tons of dried milk, blankets, shoes, soap, and medical supplies to children threatened by hunger, cold, and disease as a result of the ravages of World War II. It impressed everyone by its ability to get these vital supplies through to the children for whom they were destined—no easy task in a time when ship-loads of supplies were disappearing into black markets.

UNICEF's postwar emergency work ended around 1950. The European countries were well on the road to recovery, and UNICEF's work in mainland China had been terminated by the Communist takeover, since the Peking Government arrogantly rejected UNICEF's humanitarian work. Rather than terminating UNICEF's activities, however, the United Nations directed it to shift its attention to long-term programs for the children of the developing countries.

The United Nations believes, and the United States Government agrees, as do I, that misery among children badly prepares them for a life of free self-determination; that any improvement brought about in the standard of living during the tender formative years is apt to result in a better capacity to understand and evaluate. There is no real profit in hoping that undernourished, illiterate children will grow up to over-throw the regime under which they have suffered. There is profit in hoping that healthy, intelligent children may develop so as to exercise their God-given characteristic of the inquiring mind, and the truly inquiring mind cannot fail to see the contrast between ideologies as they affect his daily life.

In line with the General Assembly directive giving UNICEF a new lease on life, once its emergency projects were completed, the organization has launched long-term programs for children in more than 130 countries and territories, at a cost by 1965 of more than a quarter of a billion dollars. Health was the first field tackled. By 1950, most of the diseases that exacted such a fearful toll among children in the tropics and subtropics—malaria, tuberculosis, yaws, leprosy, and the like—could be cured. Working in partnership with WHO, UNICEF undertook to provide the tools—penicillin and other drugs, DDT powder, vaccines, medical instruments, dried milk. Shopping on behalf of so many nations helped UNICEF keep its costs low. Enough penicillin to cure two children of a crippling tropical disease, yaws, costs UNICEF 5 cents; enough DDT to protect seven children from malaria for a year costs UNICEF 50 cents. More than 25,000 mother and child health centers around the world have been equipped by UNICEF, and many thousands of nurses, midwives, and other health workers have been trained with the help of UNICEF grants.

Good food is even more vital to children's health than medicine. In cooperation with the FAO, UNICEF has become increasingly involved in the world-wide struggle against hunger. Beginning with shipments of skimmed milk, UNICEF soon turned to dairy-plant development. It has helped equip more than 200 modern milk plants in 40 countries. UNICEF is now helping to develop other inexpensive and nourishing foods for children, including fish flour and soy milk, and is supporting 60 "grass roots" nutrition programs based on school and community gardens. More recently, UNICEF has entered the fields of social services for children, education, and vocational training. Believing that children are a "resource" as important as a country's mines, farms, and industry,

UNICEF is working with countries around the world to protect children against the hardships of their environment and to prepare them to take their place in tomorrow's world as constructive citizens.

UNICEF's total income is now about $33 million a year. Like the Technical Assistance Fund and the Special Fund, it is what the U.N. calls an "extra-budgetary" activity. This means that its resources do not come out of the U.N.'s regular assessed budget, to which the countries are required to contribute on pain of losing their vote. Voluntary contributions from some 120 countries provide about 80 per cent of UNICEF's income. (Two top contributors, West Germany and Switzerland, are not even members of the U.N.) More than 85 of the contributors are countries in developing areas that also receive UNICEF aid. Individual contributions, including more than $2 million collected annually by children through Halloween trick-or-treat campaigns, and the proceeds from the sale of UNICEF greeting cards make up the rest of the Fund's income.

UNICEF has been able to get such good "mileage" out of its fairly modest resources because of the strong matching support it gets from the governments of beneficiary countries. The governments administer the programs; UNICEF assists and provides the staff, the buildings, and other local facilities. Over the years, local matching support has averaged $2.50 for every $1.00 provided by UNICEF. UNICEF and U.N. aid in general has gotten the results it has because it is really aid and not a handout; the countries themselves do the job, and the U.N. family helps. And its purpose is not "to win friends and influence people"—as is too often the case in country-to-country assistance programs—but to get results.

The UNICEF aid formula, as developed over the years, is to mobilize local resources through the provision of key supplies. The Technical Assistance formula, which complements the UNICEF approach, is to mobilize local resources through the advisory services of key experts.

A certain amount of modest technical assistance was provided by the U.N. out of its regular budget in the early years, and one of the main functions of the newly established specialized agencies was to provide expert assistance in such fields as health, education, and agriculture. It soon became evident, however, that not enough money could be spared from the regular budgets of the U.N. and the agencies to meet the demand for this type of aid. Accordingly, the General Assembly, in 1949, established the Expanded Program of Technical Assistance (EPTA) to finance and coordinate a greatly stepped-up effort along these lines.

Since at this writing, the scheduled merger between EPTA and the Special Fund has not yet taken place, I shall discuss the two programs separately, as they now exist.

EPTA is financed by the voluntary contributions of more than 100 countries—about $457 million was received from 1950 through 1964, with contributions now running at about $50 million a year. These contributions go into a special Technical Assistance Account, separate from the regular accounts of the U.N. and the Specialized Agencies. The Account is administered by a Technical Assistance Board consisting of a representative of the Secretary General and one representative of each of the nine Specialized Agencies participating in EPTA's work.

To summarize a rather complicated operation in a few words, the Technical Assistance Board reviews requests for assistance and decides what proportion of its total budget will go into assistance in various fields: industrial development, health, education, etc. Once this has been done, the various agencies take over, recruiting the experts and assigning them to their posts. The U.N. itself recruits and assigns experts in some of the important fields not covered by the agencies—economic planning, natural resources development, industrial development, trade promotion, public finance, statistics, public administration, and social development. EPTA also provides (through the appropriate agency channels) a considerable number of fellowships for personnel of the developing countries to study abroad and a certain amount of equipment for pilot and demonstration projects.

The U.N. Technical Assistance operation is not just a device for augmenting the resources of the various autonomous agencies in the U.N. "extended family." It brings their efforts together, too. Technical Assistance representatives are assigned to more than sixty-five countries, and they head the U.N.-family delegations to these countries. It is their job to coordinate the various forms of aid that the U.N. family provides, and since each agency has its particular interests, this is a task that requires not only professional competence but consummate diplomacy.

The U.N.'s Expanded Program of Technical Assistance, in brief, provides about $50 million a year of "muscle" for the practical work of the U.N. family. EPTA paid for the team of engineers that helped Pakistan in the final stages of constructing the great Gudda Dam to harness the Indus River. It paid the FAO experts who helped agricultural research stations in Libya triple their production; it paid the WHO staff that helped to create the Higher Institute of Nursing in Alexandria; the ILO experts who helped organize the Marine Diesel Training Center in Rangoon, where diesel engineers from all of South Asia are now being trained. More than this, it has proved that foreign aid can be a two-way proposition. In 1963, fifty-eight experts were sent to Pakistan under the program; twenty-two experts were drawn from Pakistan. Forty-seven experts were sent to Chile under the program; fifty-six were drawn from Chile. Almost every country, regardless of its stage of development, has a contribution to make to the economic and social growth of other countries. A country that is running an airport with U.N. aid may have rural education specialists who are available for service abroad. The Expanded Program of Technical Assistance facilitates this flow of knowledge and experience.

One important criticism was leveled against the very diversified technical-assistance program that developed under EPTA. Some countries claimed that valuable as the results were in particular cases, their impact was too scattered to get development projects requiring a sustaining national effort off the ground. After considerable debate in ECOSOC and the General Assembly, a new body, the United Nations Special Fund, was created in 1959 to finance large-scale "preinvestment projects."

As Paul Hoffman (now Managing Director of the Special Fund, and scheduled to head the new U.N. Development Program) has written:

> The world is rich in underutilized resources. Men are poor and go hungry while fields and pastures, lakes and oceans could feed them well. Valuable mineral deposits lie untouched beneath their feet. Forests are unexploited. Life-giving waters flow unharnessed to the sea. Scientific knowledge is but little applied. Most important of all, precious human talents and energies are wasted.

Before these resources can be tapped, surveys must be conducted, skilled technicians must be trained, and quite often, a considerable amount of applied research must be carried out. It is this "preinvestment" groundwork that must be established before real capital can be attracted.

Relying entirely on voluntary contributions from governments, the Special Fund had helped launch 421 high-priority preinvestment projects in 130 low-income countries and territories. Annual contributions to the Special Fund rose from $35.8 million in 1959 to $85.5 million in 1964. The total cost of programs approved to date comes to $919 million, with the

Special Fund putting up 60 per cent of the cost and the recipient countries the balance.

The Special Fund itself maintains only a small staff. Its programs are executed by the U.N. and nine of the Specialized Agencies. They are responsible for day-to-day supervision of project operations, the recruitment of experts, the procurement of equipment, and the placement of contracts.

At present, the Special Fund is assisting natural resources surveys and feasibility studies in 83 countries, training institutions in 71 countries, and applied research stations in 39 countries. Results are mounting, though the program is still only a few years old. A soil survey covering 620,000 acres in southern Togo has revealed extensive idle lands suitable for fruit and sugar-cane cultivation. A 150-million-ton iron ore lode has been discovered in Pakistan that will feed the country's first steel mill. A four-year search has uncovered a supply of ground water in Syria capable of irrigating 250,000 acres. Projects receiving Special Fund assistance not only are achieving their immediate objectives, but are also proving multipliers of progress. Twelve preinvestment surveys completed at a cost of $12 million have already generated $755 million of local and foreign investment. The 45,000 people trained or in training at Special Fund-assisted institutes are having an ever-widening impact on key sectors of the developing economies. More than a third are teachers and instructors who, in classrooms and workshops, are imparting practical knowledge to many times their own number. When the consolidation between the Special Fund and EPTA gets under way, the resultant Development Program should produce even more impressive fruits.

3 · War Against the Causes of War: Combined Operations

THE AGENCIES, COMMISSIONS, AND "ORGANS" described in the preceding chapter are all closely engaged in the great "War Against the Causes of War" that day in and day out is waged outside the political arena in the Glass House and throughout the world. If the relationships between the various members of the U.N.'s "extended" and "inner" families seem complicated, I can only say that the system as a whole *is* a complicated and complex one. The U.N. system was not planned as a piece; it evolved in response to the emerging needs of the postwar global society, and nothing like the coordinated development effort now being pursued by the U.N. family was even contemplated when the original machinery of the various agencies was established. Ultimately a steering committee was set up to mesh the various programs and activities of the Specialized Agencies in such a way as to minimize duplication and overlapping. This is the Administrative Committee on Coordination, whose members are the executive heads of the Specialized Agencies that have been brought into relationship with the United Nations.

The corresponding officers of agencies with which agreements are not yet in force, as well as the United Nations High Commissioner for Refugees, the Chairman of the Technical Assistance Board, the Director of the United Nations Relief and Works Agency for Palestine Refugees in the Near East, and the executive heads of other agencies within the structure of the United Nations itself, also attend the meetings.

A typical example of the coordinating function of this Committee arose during the formative stages of the IAEA. This Agency, once established, was obviously to concern itself with the peaceful uses of atomic energy, which include the areas of health, education, science, and economics. There was considerable concern and indeed some emotion among such Specialized Agencies as WHO, UNESCO, the Technical Assistance Board, and the Economic and Social Council groups that there might be encroachment on their private preserves.

The Committee on Coordination was able to work things out to such good effect that there has been virtually no encroachment and little or no friction. In matters having to do with health standards for workers in the atomic field, WHO has cooperated in their development. Training and education in atomic areas have been helped along by UNESCO. The questions of technical assistance have been cleared with the Technical Assistance Board, and so on down the line. Altogether, a very good show rather than what could have been a very sticky business.

Operating within the framework of the Committee are the consultative committees on Administrative Questions, on Statistical Matters, and on Public Information. Other bodies are established as the need arises. These include *ad hoc* technical working groups for the purpose of planning joint action in specific fields, such as migration, long-range activities for children, fundamental education, and rehabilitation of the physically handicapped.

All things considered, the system works amazingly well, and the Glass House itself functions as an effective "joint operations center." In this chapter, I shall describe the outstanding combined operations that are being conducted out of the Glass

House against poverty and hunger, the perennial enemies of mankind.

By 1960, an alarming imbalance was evident in world economic trends. In Europe and Japan, postwar recovery had been achieved more rapidly than anyone dreamed would be the case. A great wave of expanding prosperity was sweeping these and other industrialized areas, including the United States. It was as if the promise of the Industrial Revolution, so frustrated in the Depression years preceding the war, was suddenly being realized. At the same time, economic growth in Africa, Latin America, and South and Southeast Asia—the so-called underdeveloped areas—had been disappointingly slow. Far behind to begin with, the underdeveloped countries were falling further behind. Half the world's people still lived in countries where the annual per capita income was less than $100 a year. Many leading statesmen considered the growing gap in living standards between the rich and the poor countries a greater potential threat to world peace than the political disputes that usually pre-empted the headlines.

To spur concerted action in the field of development aid, the General Assembly in 1961 designated the current decade as "The United Nations Decade of Development." The goal is a 5 per cent annual rate of economic growth in the underdeveloped world. This is a modest objective if one considers that in many countries it would mean a per capita income increase of only 3 or 4 cents a year. But growth is cumulative, and if the 5 per cent target can be attained, it will at least get the process of development under way in most countries.

In accordance with Development Decade objectives, the aid given by the United Nations family of organizations is being increasingly oriented toward the foundations of development—education and training, improved health, higher agricultural yields, the introduction of appropriate scientific and technological methods, and a more rational approach to world trade. The various U.N. member governments with large country-to-country programs of their own (and in their total dollar value, these still dwarf the assistance channeled through the U.N.) are being urged to concentrate on these objectives, too, and, on the whole, their cooperation has been excellent. The developing countries, for their part, are being encouraged to concentrate on programs with a future rather than show-piece projects. Most of them—including the new African nations—now have national development plans. Often, these are unrealistic and set targets that have little chance of being attained. Through its regional economic commissions, the U.N. is giving the developing countries considerable assistance in better planning. Even when they are overly ambitious, these plans serve the valuable purpose of channeling local resources and foreign aid into programs that mean something in terms of the foundations of development.

"At the halfway point of the Decade of Development," the U.N. reported in early 1965, "a measure of progress has been achieved; while the gap in living standards remains, individual developing countries have almost certainly bettered their relative positions." The U.N., on the principle that comparisons are invidious, names no names, but a perusal of the reports of the various regional economic commissions reveals that some of the world's most strategic countries are among those that have "almost certainly bettered their relative positions." In Taiwan and in Mexico, there has been a real breakthrough toward self-sustaining economic growth, and in Thailand, Iran, and Libya, the rate of development has exceeded expectations. And while most of the developing countries remain bogged down in a vast accumulation of shortages, deficiencies, and interacting vicious circles of one kind or another, almost all of them can report heartening progress in one or two areas.

The Special Fund, with its built-in emphasis on "preinvestment," has naturally played a prominent role in the Decade of Development. The General Assembly has approved a proposal to consolidate the Special Fund and the Expanded Program of

Technical Assistance. This will make for an even more power-ful coordinated development effort. But the other agencies have also effectively shaped their programs to Development Decade objectives. The World Meteorological Organization sends experts into the jungles with rainfall gauges to measure precipitation in the catchment basins of multipurpose river-development projects. FAO experts analyze the soil to see what will grow in these same river basins. International Tele-communication Union experts draw up plans for telephone networks. WHO experts advise on what will have to be done to make project sites fit for human habitation. UNESCO plans schools, and the ILO assists in training workers for new jobs. Can radioactive isotopes or a power reactor fit into the picture? An expert recruited by the Atomic Energy Agency gives professional advice on this point.

When a young country has investigated its resources and drawn up a plan for developing them, how can it obtain the funds to translate blueprints into power plants, factories, refineries, railways, farm-to-market roads, and water systems? The "consortium approach" to development financing is one solution that is currently being explored. United Nations lend-ing agencies put up some of the capital; and member govern-ments supply some funds themselves under their regular for-eign-aid programs and encourage private investors to furnish additional amounts. One example of this combined approach can be seen on an island in the Niger River, 260 miles north of Lagos, where work is progressing on a multipurpose dam that has been called the cornerstone of Nigeria's current six-year development plan.

There, on Kainji Island, a project has been worked out with United Nations assistance for a 215-foot-high dam across the valley, with a power station to generate electricity for Ni-geria's growing needs and with transmission lines to help create a nationwide network. A 100-mile-long reservoir be-hind the dam will provide a controlled source of water for surrounding farms, in place of the alternating floods and droughts of former years, and reservoir fisheries will add to the country's supply of high-protein foods.

A survey financed with the help of the Special Fund showed that the Kainji Island project was perfectly feasible and well worth the $200 million it would cost. But how could that amount be raised by a country whose average income per person was only about $100 a year? The answer was in joint financing. Nigeria itself will provide about one-fourth of the total. The World Bank will supply $82 million under a thirty-five-year loan, with seven commercial banks participating. The rest will be lent by Italy, the Netherlands, the United Kingdom, the United States, and perhaps additional countries.

Dams and powerhouses are the "spectaculars" among development projects, but they are only one aspect of the kind of balanced development the U.N. is trying to encourage during the present decade. One of the most important lessons that was learned from postwar reconstruction in Europe and the early attempts to initiate growth in the less-developed countries was the overriding importance of the human element in economic progress. European reconstruction succeeded so well because all that was necessary was to rebuild the "plant." The scientists, the technicians, the skilled workers—the human resources indispensable to a modern economy—were there. Once the European factories were rebuilt, workers as efficient as any in the world streamed to them and production skyrocketed. In the developing countries, on the other hand, the "personnel problem" soon proved to be one of the principal obstacles to economic growth. Unemployment was high, but key positions in new industries remained vacant because of a lack of qualified applicants. Fewer than half the children had schools of any sort to go to, and fewer than 10 per cent received any secondary education or vocational training. Even the efficiency of unskilled labor was low, owing to the effects of disease and malnutrition.

For this reason, investment in people—health, education, training—emerged as one of the most important aspects of the Development Decade. One of the most notable successes of the Decade to date has been the stepped-up rate of training and educational assistance. New institutions are now turning out thousands of teachers, doctors, nurses, technicians, skilled workers, managers, and administrators. A foreign expert serving under the Expanded Program of Technical Assistance does not complete his mission satisfactorily until he has trained his own replacement. The era of foreign management is rapidly passing in the developing countries, as it must if these countries are to stand on their own feet.

An example of how the Development Decade approach affects the work of a particular agency can be seen in the case of UNICEF, the United Nations Children's Fund. Prior to 1960, UNICEF aid was largely restricted to child health and nutrition. This humanitarian program had important implications for the kind of "human resource development" called for in the Development Decade, but it was evident that it did not go far enough if children were to be thought of not just as children, but as tomorrow's citizens. In 1961, UNICEF broadened its field of aid to include education, vocational training and social services to help children and their families bridge the gap between old and new ways of life. Many of the projects it is now assisting are specifically designed to prepare children to participate in their countries' future development. In collaboration with UNESCO, for example, UNICEF is helping the government of Thailand extend its system of universal primary education from four to seven years. It is also helping the Thai Government introduce practical courses in manual arts and agriculture into the primary curriculum. In India, UNICEF and the ILO are working with the government on a project to provide vocational training to children who drop out of school after the primary grades. As a further step along Development Decade lines, UNICEF is now sponsoring a series of regional seminars to see how programs for children can be integrated into the mainstream of broader development efforts. All these activities reflect UNICEF's new motto: "We must prepare as well as protect the child."

Comparable to the Decade of Development effort in scope —and in urgency—is the world-wide Freedom From Hunger Campaign, launched by the FAO in 1960. For this "joint operation," the FAO's Rome headquarters is the nerve center. But the problem of feeding mankind's rapidly increasing numbers is such a critical one, both for the present and for the future, that it has become one of the leading concerns of the entire U.N. "development team." The Special Fund, the International Development Association, and UNICEF have a heavy financial involvement in the campaign. WHO, which regards malnutrition as the world's most widespread disease and one that is just as devastating in its effects as malaria or tuberculosis, has become increasingly active in the fight. The International Meteorological Organization, by helping take some of the guesswork out of weather prediction, and the IAEA, by supplying radioactive tracer elements for agricultural research, are helping the developing countries establish food production on a more scientific basis. It is the responsibility of the U.N. Population Commission to estimate how many mouths there will be to feed by the end of the century, and the Commission's conservative estimate—6 to 7 billion— has done much to jolt the nations of the world into full awareness of the seriousness of the food problem.

By 1960, it was evident that in the poorer countries agricultural development was lagging even more seriously than industrial development. While the U.S., Japan, Canada, Western Europe, and Australia were setting new production records almost every year and wondering what to do with their surpluses, per capita food output in much of Asia, Africa, and Latin America remained almost stagnant. While a quarter of the world's people worried about their expanding waistlines, the remaining three-quarters worried about obtaining enough food to keep body and soul together.

It was not difficult to account for the growing disparity in the state of agriculture between the industrialized and the developing countries. In the former, agriculture had become a scientifically oriented industry. Years of experimentation with fertilizers, new strains of crops, animal breeding, and animal nutrition were paying off. Machines were replacing farm hands—and doing their work more efficiently. In the developing countries, agriculture was not an industry; it was a way of life for 80 to 90 per cent of the inhabitants. Most of them continued to farm the land as their parents and grandparents had done. Vital nitrates and other mineral elements were taken out of the soil every year, and they were not replaced. In one of the Andean countries in South America, farmers sold the biggest potatoes to the city markets and kept the small ones for seed. Not surprisingly, the potatoes kept getting smaller and smaller.

The Freedom From Hunger effort has two general objectives: to increase agricultural production by establishing farming in the developing countries on a more scientific basis, and to improve levels of nutrition by teaching people to grow and to use the specific foods required for good health. These objectives are equally vital. Day in and day out, the majority of people in Asia, Africa, and Latin America do not get enough food, purely in terms of calories, to perform a hard day's work efficiently. As one Indian villager told a visitor: "I do not know whether I could work harder if I had as much to eat as I wanted. I have never had more than two meals a day." Furthermore, the diet of the average person in these areas is largely confined to one or two starchy staples—rice, corn, or wheat. Meat, eggs, and garden vegetables seldom find their way into rural family diets except on feast days. Such supplies as are available are taken to town and sold. As a consequence, at least half the world's population suffers from chronic malnutrition. Young children, who need proteins and other body-building foods so desperately, are, tragically, the hardest hit. No one who has seen a child of one or two dying of protein malnutrition can ever forget the sight—the puffy, waterlogged tiny body; the blotchy skin; and the terrible expression of misery and apathy in the eyes.

New irrigation works and large-scale land-reclamation projects are gradually increasing the total acreage under cultivation throughout the world, but not nearly at the rate the earth's population is growing. The real hope is to increase the productivity of existing farmlands in the developing countries. The potential is enormous, for in general, in these countries, agricultural yields are no higher than they were in Europe during Roman times or the early Middle Ages.

The answer to growing *more* food in the developing countries is increased use of fertilizers, better seeds, better strains of livestock, up-to-date methods of cultivation—and, most important of all, progressive farmers. The attack on rural illiteracy and ignorance is, in fact, the key to the whole Freedom From Hunger effort. One of the most encouraging signs of basic progress in recent years has been the success of certain countries in building up their rural school systems and in strengthening their agricultural-extension services.

There is an old Chinese proverb that says: "Give a man a fish and you feed him for one day; teach him to catch fish and you feed him for life." The best way to teach is by demonstration, and most of the specific field projects that have been launched under the Freedom From Hunger Campaign are demonstration projects. Many of these demonstration projects have been supported not only by the FAO and the other agencies but by individuals, business firms, and church and civic groups. Several hundred fertilizer companies in North America, Europe, and Japan have financed a $1-million World Fertilizer Program, which has put on more than 11,000 demonstrations witnessed by half a million farmers. Yields on experimental plots show increases of as much as 87 per cent, and the tall, healthy plants on fertilized plots, growing alongside the scrawny specimens in nonfertilized fields, are dramatic evidence to the local farmers of the effect of a sound fertilizer program.

In the tropical depths of eastern Nigeria, five Norwegian families are demonstrating methods of growing better crops, raising healthy poultry and farm animals, and purifying the water supply. The half million farmers in the district will be encouraged to use seeds from these crops so that the experiment, jointly sponsored by FAO and the Norwegian Church Relief Fund, may continue.

Not only the land but the sea is a resource that is underused in the developing countries. In the past, Ceylon imported three-quarters of its fish, even though the country had 90,000 fishermen and good offshore fishing grounds. The difficulty was that with their primitive catamarans (log rafts with a sail), the fishermen could not reach the best fishing-grounds and seldom brought home more than 15 pounds of fish. Now, under the Freedom From Hunger Campaign, 200 catamarans have been equipped with outboard motors that carry them into waters where a 150-pound catch is not unusual.

Since children are the principal victims of malnutrition, it is only natural that special efforts to improve children's diets figure prominently in the Freedom From Hunger effort. UNICEF, working closely with FAO and WHO, is aiding grass-roots "applied nutrition" projects in seventy countries. The idea behind these applied nutrition programs is that even the poorest rural families can improve the quality of their diet through "do it yourself" efforts, if they are given the right kind of help and instruction to get things started.

The largest of these projects is the All-India Applied Nutrition Program, which grew out of an experiment begun in 1959 in one of India's poorer states, Orissa. At the time, there was hardly a child among the poorer families in Orissa who did not show symptoms of protein malnutrition or vitamin deficiency. Practically all the available land was taken up in rice or millet cultivation; there seemed to be no way of improving the quality of the diet without cutting down on the quantity available. FAO advisers and local officials hit on a plan, however. There were thousands of irrigation ponds scattered over the countryside that could be used to raise fish. And many of the villagers kept poultry of a nondescript sort. The birds laid few eggs, but if the villagers could be provided with blooded birds and taught how to care for them, egg production would shoot up. Further, despite the shortage of land, a careful survey turned up a quarter acre here and a quarter acre there that could be spared to grow garden vegetables.

The Orissa government, with UNICEF aid, stocked up on fish nets, garden seeds, and chicken wire and started out to see what could be done. Hundreds of thousands of fishes were distributed from government hatcheries and planted in irrigation ponds. Tens of thousands of leghorn chicks were hatched and released in village poultry runs. The larger landowners were approached to donate land for gardens. The project really began to move when the village women were brought into it. The men saw little need to modify their traditional practices. The women, who for generations had watched the children they so painfully bore sicken and die, were the responsive ones. Applied-nutrition workers scored their "sociological breakthrough" in Orissa when they began organizing village women's clubs and giving them the responsibility for planting gardens, raising fish and poultry, and preparing special meals once or twice a week for the children and pregnant woman of the community. The men learned the value of the new foods by seeing what they accomplished for their wives and children, and soon they began to cooperate too. School gardens provided another important approach to "learning by doings." In Orissa, the school garden, where each child has his own tiny experimental plot, now serves not only as a source of production for protective foods, but as an ideal rural science lab to reach tomorrow's farmers.

The "Orissa approach" has now been extended to all of India. UNICEF is involved to the extent of about $10 million in supplies, equipment, and stipends for the training of extension workers. The voluntary Freedom From Hunger committees of Australia and New Zealand are contributing to the program as well. The federal and state governments of India will, of course, provide services costing many times as much before the program is finished. Despite the fact that India itself will eventually bear the principal burden of its costs, the All-India Applied Nutrition Program is an important landmark in international cooperation, for without UNICEF supplies and without FAO technical assistance, the program would certainly not have gotten under way in such a short period of time; it might never have gotten under way at all. The results thus far are not spectacular, viewed in the perspective of India's great need, but they are some cause for hope. Children in some areas where poultry raising has been inaugurated are getting a ration of half an egg a week. This is painfully little, but it is a great deal if we remember that, for a thousand years, the ancestors of these children may not have tasted an egg. The first step is the most important because it is the hardest.

Five years after the beginning of the Freedom From Hunger Campaign, the balance sheet is a mixed one. One of the purposes of the Campaign was "to bring to the attention of mankind the seriousness of the situation and thus create a climate of informed opinion favorable to the launching of an all-out attack on the problem." This has certainly been accomplished. Individual projects have shown *what* can be done and *how* it can be done. But the statistics on over-all food production, which are analyzed every year by FAO's statisticians in Rome, remain discouraging. In the Far East and Latin America, there is not as much food available per person as there was prior to World War II. Protein deficiency remains the world's No. 1 nutritional problem, and to overcome it, the supply of animal protein—meat, fish, eggs, milk—in the developing countries will have to increase fivefold by the end of this century, according to the latest FAO estimates. There is hope that this may not have to be literally the case. The international agencies are working with the scientific establishments in many countries to develop cheap animal-protein substitutes based on such products as cottonseed, soybeans, and peanuts, and the results to date are decidedly encouraging. But as the FAO has pointed out, for these vastly increased supplies of high-quality protein, in whatever form, to become available "entails the application of science and technology to the world's agriculture on a hitherto unprecedented scale."

Still, the population of Asia, Africa, and Latin America has been increasing at the rate of about 45 million persons a year since 1960. Even a dead heat in the race between population and food production in these areas is a "moral victory," so to speak. Moreover, many of the major Freedom From Hunger efforts initiated over the past five years are just beginning to pay off. Prospects may well improve when the impact of these efforts begins to be felt. In any event, I hesitate to imagine what the prospects would be, had this international campaign never been launched.

One thing that can be said for the postwar world is that it has seen no actual large-scale famines of the kind that used to devastate whole countries. The Bengal famine of World War II, which claimed several million victims (no one really knows how many millions), was the last in modern times. Postwar food surpluses in the economically advanced countries have provided a cushion against famine. Shipments of surplus food from the economically advanced countries have kept India and other countries going despite several series of bad farm years. For a number of years, U.N. officials speculated on the idea of using agricultural surpluses from the developed countries, not merely to keep the underdeveloped countries from starving, but to promote the modernization of agriculture and other productive undertakings.

The World Food Program, launched in 1961, is an attempt to use surplus food as one of the basic tools in the U.N. development effort. Close to seventy nations have donated surplus foodstuffs, services (mainly shipping), and cash to the value of $92 million. The surplus foods are used to pay part of the salaries of people working on irrigation, roads, and other labor-intensive projects. Since most of their pay would go for food in any event, the arrangement is a beneficial one all around. World Food Program resources are supporting a major agricultural resettlement project in Ghana, a virgin-land project in Tanganyika, and a project to reclaim 1,000 acres of tidal land on Taiwan. Other projects include the production of improved animal food in India, the rehabilitation of eroded pasture lands in Chile, and the construction of roads to link forty-seven Turkish villages to the national highway network. This use of agricultural surpluses from abroad to help people reduce their dependence on such surpluses is certainly one of the most creative and imaginative foreign-aid formulas ever devised.

At least 80 per cent of the news that gets printed about the U.N. concerns its political wrangles and debates, although in reality about 80 per cent of the organization's efforts are devoted to economic and social matters concerning which there is little controversy. Bad news, of course, drives out good news. My own training and experience has been primarily political, and because of this fact, my emphasis in this book is on the political processes in the Glass House. I only hope that this chapter and the previous one will serve to refute the commonly held opinion that the U.N. is "just a debating society." It is far more than that. It is an organization that gets things done and that gets them done well. If not in the political field, at least in the economic and social field, it has persuaded "the lion to lie down with the lamb"—an accomplishment that had previously eluded mankind. The Soviet Union and other Soviet-bloc countries participate in the deliberations of ECOSOC, the majority of the specialized agencies, and the "inner family" organizations, such as the Special Fund and UNICEF. They contribute financially to these organizations and support their work wholeheartedly. If a political settlement of the Cold War still seems far distant, an amicable truce has, at any rate, been worked out within the U.N. family, so far as economic and social matters go. Maurice Pate, the first Executive Director of UNICEF, whose death in January, 1965, was such a loss to the international community, used to say: "When I look into the eyes of a hungry child, I don't ask about his politics." The U.N.'s humanitarian endeavors have always been carried out in this spirit, and I trust they always will be.

I have by no means described all the activities of the U.N. and the U.N. family in the War Against the Causes of War. To give some idea of how the system as a whole works, I have concentrated on the major development programs the U.N. family has sponsored. Besides this, of course, the U.N. has acted as the conscience of mankind in a number of matters. The Universal Declaration of Human Rights, approved unanimously by the General Assembly in 1948, codifies ideals toward which the human race has been painfully groping for thousands of years. Under the guidance of the twenty-one-member Commission on Human Rights, established in 1948, international conventions outlawing genocide, protecting refugees, and ensuring the political rights of women have been adopted by the U.N. and have entered into force.

Other important aspects of the Commission's work are carried on by the Subcommission on Prevention of Discrimination and Protection of Minorities. It will be remembered that in 1964 the Subcommission members were invited to visit

Atlanta, Georgia, to see for themselves the attempts being made in at least one Southern city toward peaceful integration. The newspaper accounts indicate that the trip was at least partially successful and that the members came away much impressed by the progress made, in spite of demonstrations put on for their "edification." This must have been a welcome change from the futility and frustration that seem the inevitable lot of this Subcommission.

In the exploration of the urgent scientific problems confronting humanity, the U.N. system also functions as a meeting ground for the world's best minds. Through its Scientific Advisory Committee and similar organs, the U.N. has sponsored two international conferences on the peaceful uses of atomic energy and two conferences on unconventional sources of energy. The conferences on unconventional energy considered everything from solar cookers to volcanic steam. In 1963, a mammoth U.N. Conference on the Application of Science and Technology for the Benefit of the Less Developed Areas took place in Geneva with 1,665 participants from 96 countries. In 1965 alone, major conferences were scheduled on population, desalinization of water, and the prevention of crime.

On the political front, the United Nations "presence" has been used on a mere handful of occasions. In the War Against the Causes of War, the United Nations "presence" can be seen around the world. On a typical day, we could imagine ourselves starting at the International Date Line and moving west: First, we might find a WHO worker investigating tuberculosis in Samoa. We could move on to see a midwife in Thailand pedaling a UNICEF bicycle to a remote village to deliver a baby. At Chittagong, the port of East Pakistan, we could watch a UNICEF supply officer as he checks a cargo of nutrition supplies that is being unloaded. In New Delhi, the FAO representative confers with a high government official on the place of agriculture in the new five-year plan. In the highlands of East Africa, another FAO expert sets out by jeep to study cattle diseases. An industrial-development consultant in Nigeria looks over the plans for a new factory. A representative of the Atomic Energy Agency watches while scientists in São Paulo, Brazil, activate a new research reactor. In Peru, an International Labour Organisation expert inspects a training center for Andean Indians. The elevation is 14,000 feet, and it is hard for him to catch his breath, but he is gratified to see that the various power tools have been properly oiled and sharpened.

As Walter Lippmann said, in an address delivered at the United Nations in March, 1965, the world is on the threshold of a "great revolution"—perhaps the greatest revolution in the history of mankind. Science and technology have given us the weapons to wipe out all the poverty, all the hunger, and the greater part of the sickness in the world. In so doing, we can only hope those forces have shown us the way toward international cooperation in pursuit of the goals that are within our grasp. It is in the matter of international cooperation toward peaceful objectives that I think the U.N. has had its greatest success. And when the current political debates in the General Assembly and the Security Council have subsided, I believe that this cooperation will be acknowledged as the U.N.'s greatest achievement in the first twenty years of its existence.

4 · Perennial Challenges

T HE POLITICAL DEBATES that consume much of the time and energy of the Assembly and Security Council give rise to a number of challenges to the U.N.'s decisions, its *modus operandi*, and sometimes to its very existence. International political analysts have utilized many hundred thousands of words to describe, criticize, or justify these challenges. It is with some trepidation that I suggest that the major reason underlying virtually all of these challenges can be oversimplified into one word. When applied to international usage, that word is "sovereignty"; when translated into its simplest terms, that word is "selfishness."

All nations that have joined the United Nations since its beginning have come in under the provisions of Article 4 of the Charter, which provides that a nation making application must be "peace-loving" and must in addition declare itself "willing and able" to discharge the obligations of membership in the international fellowship. Each member nation in the United Nations today has made this solemn pledge, and each nation still outside the international family appears to be ready to make the same pledge in the event it could be admitted to membership. *Yet all of them, without exception, reserve to themselves the right (usually openly) to wage war, impose or join blockades, indulge in subversive propaganda against other*

94

governments, and many other activities of questionable propriety, if they feel that it will serve their best interests to do so. Herein lies the major challenge and the greatest difficulty facing a viable international organization such as the United Nations hopes to be: that international cooperation must live despite the selfish interests of some 117 sovereign nations, each strongly jealous of its own prestige.

I have noted of late that certain critics of the United Nations have tended to charge the newly emergent countries with being the outstanding exponents of hypernationalism. Many of them are—in fact, many of them would never have emerged into independence had they not burned with a strong nationalistic fervor. On the other hand, these particular critics tend to forget or ignore the fact that many older, well-established, proud nations can exhibit equal fervor in their own interests. Certainly the United Kingdom, France, Italy, and the United States, to say nothing of the East European and North African blocs, have many times demonstrated their readiness to challenge the dicta of the General Assembly or the Security Council when they felt that their own interests were being jeopardized.

And so we move inevitably from the word "selfishness" to the word "defiance," which in itself creates something of a paradox. You might normally say that if someone thoroughly disapproved of an organization to which he belonged, he would in all probability resign from it, but the United Nations is not in that category. Over and over again, through the years since San Francisco, many of the members have regularly challenged the authority and propriety of United Nations decisions and recommendations, but only once, so far as I am aware, has any present member (namely, Indonesia) withdrawn from the organization, and no applicant for membership has withdrawn its application. Why do all nations apparently want to join the United Nations? Some, like the Communist Chinese regime, do so in the full knowledge that they will be members of a hopeless minority from the stand-point of voting strength. Others, such as the new nations emerging from colonialism, realize that they have much to learn and will have to serve a considerable apprenticeship before obtaining much influence in the world body. Although still others may wish to shun the Cold War quarrels that mar each session, all want to join, and to date, only Sukarno's Indonesia has chosen to leave, which should give pause to the critics who have prematurely proclaimed the early collapse of the organization. And there are already indications that many Indonesians regret the intemperate reaction of their Bung—although there are no indications that the abortive coup of October, 1965, had any connection with such a reaction.

There are many reasons why members have not wished to leave the United Nations, even for a short time. Many of them refuse to do this because they feel that, in spite of its shortcomings and in spite of the actions it may take that they themselves do not particularly like, there is over-all a greater value to remaining in that body than in putting oneself outside the pale. Even a temporary and limited withdrawal may prove unwise. This has been particularly true in one or two cases—notably when the Soviet Union walked out of the Security Council in 1950 just before the resolutions on the Korean conflict calling for collective action on the part of the United Nations. Since that day no Soviet representative has ever left the chamber of either the Security Council or the General Assembly, or any of the other organs of the organization.

The French walked out of the General Assembly in 1955, I remember, because they insisted that Algeria should not be discussed in the General Assembly since the difficulty was purely internal. Other countries have threatened to withdraw, such as South Africa, because of the General Assembly's insistence on passing resolutions against apartheid. However, most of the nations who find fault with the United Nations content themselves with challenging the jurisdiction and the right of the United Nations to pass such resolutions and to indulge in such discussions. Often they disobey or ignore the recommendations. They know perhaps that it would be foolhardy for them to leave this great international organization, and find themselves on the outside with few, if any, friends and with little or no influence on international matters. It is entirely true that if one should leave an organization of this sort permanently, one in fact leaves the field of struggle to the enemy. It is surely one of the major reasons why the United States should never leave the United Nations as long as there is a possibility for that organization to continue in existence. If the United States should withdraw from the United Nations, the Soviet Union would then be the most powerful country in the organization and, therefore, in command of the field. It would certainly not be a wise thing either for us or for the rest of the world to take a chance on that eventuality.

Defiance of the United Nations as a result of hypersovereignty can be jurisdictional, financial, military, political, or a combination of all four. Regardless of the basic reason for defiance, it does in the long run tend to have a weakening effect on the organization. There are times, of course, when certain types of defiance have caused at least a temporary strengthening of international cooperation on the part of other members of the United Nations. As examples, one might cite Korea, where sixteen nations held together with increasing solidity in the face of Communist political attack; Palestine, where a large percentage of the members of the General Assembly became more and more concerned with both Arab and Israeli defiance; and the Congo, wherein internal dissension and Communist sniping served to solidify the determination of the Secretary General and of an overwhelming majority of the General Assembly that a strong position was needed. These examples do not, however, weaken the overall statement that defiance tends to have a bad effect on the

United Nations' structure as a whole. Obviously, answers must be found to a great many problems that are not always possible within the United Nations family. If the defiance had not been already declared or anticipated, one might have hoped that such situations as those of Southeast Asia, Kashmir, disarmament, a nuclear test-ban treaty, and even the dispute over West Irian might have found a more comfortable berth for treatment in the General Assembly sessions. As is known, none of these questions has been settled by the United Nations per se, and whatever settlements have been made have occurred outside its walls.

I have mentioned the major reasons for defiance of the United Nations because of sovereignty. Jurisdictional defiance usually comes as a result of a clash of interpretation between the more emotional or humanitarian position and the provisions of Article 2, Chapter 7, of the United Nations Charter. Here is the core of that section of the Charter.

> Nothing contained in the present Charter shall authorize the United Nations to intervene in matters which are essentially within the domestic jurisdiction of any state or shall require the members to submit such matters to settlement under the present Charter; but this principle shall not prejudice the application of enforcement measures under Chapter 7.

Over the past sixteen years, there have been many sharp disagreements based upon the belief of the accused member that the subject of the accusation was purely an internal and domestic matter and as such was none of the United Nations' business. Many of the colonialism debates over the years have been clouded by this argument, and I have already mentioned an occasion on which the delegates of the accused country formally arose and walked out of the General Assembly, refusing to participate either in the debate or in the vote on a matter they considered to be totally within their own domestic jurisdiction.

These actions have been subjected to criticism in varying degrees over the years, but it is obvious that the governments concerned were faced with what they considered a serious challenge to their own rights of self-government, and they reacted as if the United Nations were deliberately and maliciously meddling in their internal affairs. I have often wondered what the United States would have done in the event that some African nation brought forward an item on the subject of Little Rock, Arkansas, or Oxford, Mississippi. It might have been possible for trouble-makers to launch unfounded accusations concerning the relations of the United States with Puerto Rico or with Hawaii before the latter became a full-fledged state of the union. Certain it is that from time to time other nations that have given lip service to the anticolonialism drive have convicted themselves of the same sort of attitude. A typical example is the refusal of the Soviet Union to pay any attention to the resolutions on Hungary in the General Assembly. Morocco claimed Mauritania as part of its own territory and denied that the Mauritanians had any right to independence. The Arab League refuses to recognize the validity of the State of Israel, and continues to threaten to drive that infant nation into the sea. Hence, although colonialism in the main has been a word applied almost exclusively to West European nations, there is considerable room for skepticism on the point. If all nations were utterly candid on the matter, they would have to admit that there have been times in their history when they themselves, regardless of present position, would have been inclined to rest their case on the concept of the inviolability of domestic jurisdiction expressed in Article 2, Chapter 7.

Financial defiance has derived from several reasons, but usually they are more open than the jurisdictional and political cases. Article 2, Chapter 7, again appears occasionally, but more often we find examples of legalistic interpretations as to political disagreement, as to action taken, and some recognizable cases of mischief-making and pure political "agin-ism." The year 1962 saw an acceleration of financial defiance— particularly from the standpoint of paying the costs of such operations as those of UNEF in Palestine and ONUC in the Congo. By January 1, 1963, eighteen member nations of the United Nations had deliberately refused to pay their assessments in one or both of these two operations. Generally speaking, the groups were made up of the Soviet bloc and the Arab League, but there were one or two notable exceptions, whose inclusion is not only well known but in some cases understandable. In August, 1965, the twelve nations who continued to refuse to pay any of these costs were:

	UNEF (Palestine)	ONUC (Congo)	Amount Owed
Albania	x	x	$ 95,972
Byelorussian S.S.R.	x	x	2,107,165
Cuba	x	x	690,633
Czechoslovakia	x	x	4,069,683
France		x	17,752,565
Hungary	x	x	2,257,074
Poland	x	x	4,322,387
Romania	x	x	926,994
South Africa		x	1,117,647
Ukrainian S.S.R.	x	x	8,049,135
U.S.S.R.	x	x	62,236,882
Yemen	x	x	127,129

The position of most of the Soviet bloc in following the Russian lead is not hard to understand. The Soviets take the position that France, Israel, and the United Kingdom should pay all the costs of UNEF because they invaded Egypt, and that the Congo operation is illegal because it was ordered by the General Assembly rather than the Security Council. On the other hand, why is only Yemen of the Arab League refusing to pay its share of the Palestine operation?

Article 19, to which I have referred, provides that any member that lags more than two years behind in payment of its dues may lose its vote in the General Assembly. Since all of the delinquent nations listed are in the habit of paying their administrative assessments with promptness, a situation of this kind did not arise for any of them until the fall of 1964.

The few times in the past when member nations of the United Nations have become ineligible under Article 19 of the Charter for a vote in the General Assembly, the matter has been handled with discretion and has not been made a matter of public discussion. The following is the technique: The Secretary General, or his representative, calls in the Permanent Representative of the country concerned and advises him that the country is now a full two years behind in its obligations to the organization and that, consequently, the Secretary General will not be allowed under Article 19 to include that nation in the next roll call taken in the General Assembly. The Representative himself is advised that it would be less embarrassing if he should absent himself from the chamber until the delinquency is made up, because questions might arise as to why the name of his country was not called. In such cases the member nation is merely noted as "absent."

I can assure you that this technique was extremely successful up until the latest crisis. Without exception, the Representative concerned got in touch with his government on an emergency basis, and funds were forthcoming, thus restoring the nation's eligibility to vote. It would seem to me that this is a good way of handling the matter from the standpoint of prestige, but I have always felt that a system somewhat akin to the posting system used by most social clubs would also have great value. Occasionally, one sees a list in the Congressional Record or elsewhere that shows the delinquencies of the various countries. This, however, gains no wide publicity, and it would seem to me that the pride of each member nation would be very much at stake if such a list were openly posted in the Glass House. I do not know whether this will ever be done—but I believe it could be effective.

This Article 19 business, basically back of all the defiance of financing due to political ploys, is not as simple as many—myself included—have tried to make it seem. There is without doubt a serious legal question: that of the right of the General Assembly under the Charter to take over such powers from the Security Council. The Soviets and the French and the rest deny that such powers exist; they maintain that only the Council can authorize such expenditures as those for peace-keeping operations. The reaction of the International Court of Justice was strong but not unanimous (9 to 5) and at all events was merely an advisory opinion, not technically carrying the force of law.

More important, in the judgment of many observers, was the General Assembly's acceptance by a three-to-one margin of the opinions as binding. Yet some legal people tell us that if the Assembly had no power to make these appropriations in the first place (which is still moot), then they would certainly have no power to approve the advisory opinion of the ICJ in the second place. What is obviously needed, among other things, is some sort of an adjudication of the matter by due legal process and in unmistakable terms.

Apart from all this, the fact remains that powerful members of the United Nations are resolved to refuse to be bound by United Nations actions, recommendations, or resolutions if they feel that such are not in their interest. I stress elsewhere, notably in Chapter 7, that the United States literally cannot be forced by the Glass House to do anything she doesn't want to do. Small nations quite rightly feel the same way. If, therefore, the General Assembly should vote to approve an advisory opinion of the ICJ which is inimical to the interests of the United States, we would obviously ignore the whole thing.

I feel that this realization was a strong factor in the apparent reversal of the U.S. position in this regard, announced in mid-August by Ambassador Goldberg as a happy omen for his tenure at the United Nations. In the statement we renewed our allegiance to Article 19, but frankly and ruefully agreed that we didn't have the votes to make it stick. With equal candor (and I applaud this as much as the so-called concession) we made it clear that the United States would follow a similar policy of nonpayment in the event of the General Assembly's taking an action of which we did not approve.

This puts the matter squarely on the line and must, I believe, bring a final order out of chaotic inaction. Meanwhile, my applause for the realistic attitude taken by Washington.

The reasons for defiance of the United Nations in financial matters are thus quite often recognizable; serious poverty is rarely the reason for a government's delinquency. The poorest countries have very small assessments indeed, inasmuch as the rate or ratio of assessment is invariably tied to the ability to pay, and reviewed each year by the Administrative Committee of the General Assembly.

Any country having really serious financial difficulties can present the argument to the General Assembly that its assessment should be cut or adjusted in some way, and it is very rare indeed that the poorer countries are asked to pay more than they can actually afford. There is, of course, an ominous future for the United Nations if some way is not found to stimulate willing payment.

Purely military defiance of the United Nations is extremely rare. Most of the defiance having to do with the use of troop engagements, both bilateral and multilateral, is based on political considerations, but there have been cases where nonmembers, such as North Korea and Communist China, have defied the United Nations from a military standpoint and in fact have waged war against U.N. troops. The military potential of the United Nations is never wholly secure for reasons of sovereignty and money and internal U.N. politics. For example, no troops from permanent members of the Security Council are asked for by the Secretary General when the United Nations needs military personnel. It has been considered, I think wisely, that where Cold War difficulties around the world call for U.N. action, it would be far better if Russian and United States troops were not present. There have also been other considerations: It would have been obviously unpalatable for the United Nations to utilize United States troops in the question of Suez. Even though there was no direct fighting between United Nations troops and the French and British, this might have developed, and it was obviously in the best interest of the Western alliance and the United Nations to avoid such a confrontation. By the same token it would be out of the question to have Soviet troops in the United Nations forces where the quarrel might be between one of the Soviet's allies and the United Nations. Therefore, it has been more or less agreed, although I know of no resolution on the subject, that the larger countries, militarily speaking, such as the United States and the Soviet Union, are called upon only for logistic support or transport and occasionally for weapons, but never for men.

When we come to the question of political defiance against the United Nations, either of resolutions or of actions, one can indeed make up a long list. I will not weary you with such a recital, but a few typical examples should illustrate the point.

Over the years since 1947, there has been a great amount of defiance from both the Arabs and Israelis on the Palestine question. Both India and Pakistan have defied United Nations resolutions calling upon them to negotiate their dispute over Kashmir, and statements by Shastri and Ayub Khan following the "undeclared war" show that neither harbors any idea of compromise. The Soviet Union has refused even to consider United Nations resolutions having to do with Hungary. South Africa has refused to recognize or consider U.N. resolutions having to do with apartheid or any of its other racial difficulties, such as its treatment of people of Indian origin. So defiance, as one can see, runs all the way from waging war against the United Nations—that is, actually shooting at United

Nations troops—to refusal to participate in U.N. debates. In between these two there are many shades of political gray. One could say perhaps that even the Soviet campaign for their three-headed Secretary Generalship, which we came to call the "troika" back in 1960, could be characterized as a defiance of the United Nations. Certainly it was in defiance of established order and the Charter of the United Nations, which calls for a single Secretary General, to be free from political pressure of any kind. And, it is definitely in defiance of common sense.

Sometimes nations announce in advance that they will pay no attention to projected General Assembly resolutions or actions. Some, secure in the foreknowledge of a veto, have warned of their decision not to recognize certain resolutions or actions of the Security Council. Some have so defied the Trusteeship Council and the Economic and Social Council, in which no veto procedure exists. So the whole picture is a very complicated one—a picture of more than a hundred nations— some giving only lip service to certain kinds of General Assembly action, dozens abstaining because of unwillingness to take sides, and a fairly solid majority that can normally be expected to vote their firm convictions. Once in a while you find one or more of the latter identifying themselves as defiant, and truly the defiant ones must be considered courageous whether one agrees with them or not.

A massive percentage of the time of the United Nations and of its various organs must be taken up with efforts to persuade the blunt, courageous, and sometimes wrongly opinionated that it is to their interest to support the United Nations. Without them, the organization cannot survive. Even with them, the cards often seem stacked against the organization. It is a never-ending struggle that seems to stretch out ahead of the planners of world cooperation.

There are other ways in which dissident elements can and do challenge the very existence as well as the decisions of the

United Nations. Side-issue sallies may be made within the Specialized Agencies and the special boards, commissions, and committees of the organization. Such matters as Chinese representation, for instance, are brought forward in these boards, commissions, and agencies over and over again in spite of the annual and overriding decisions of the General Assembly. Here, by a series of flank attacks, the Communists probe for weak spots in the free-world line. They ignore the fact that the parent body has already ruled on the matter. Although such moves have been regularly defeated by the alertness of the delegates concerned and occasionally by noncommitted officers of such bodies, this does not mean that the attempt will be abandoned. There is always the possibility that in the more liberally oriented agencies some carelessness or personal opinion shift might result in some significant change of vote in an international organization. Such a change might give people the erroneous idea that sentiment in international organizations is leaning toward a more lenient position in respect to the Communist Chinese regime than the General Assembly's actions indicate.

Now why do we have all these different challenges? Do the challengers sincerely wish to destroy the organization? I remember very solemnly and sincerely accusing the Soviet Union in the fall of 1960, during the notorious shoe-pounding days, of a policy of rule or ruin. I thought then that Khrushchev had deliberately set out to debase the General Assembly in the eyes of the world by playing the buffoon (and being successful, in part at least). His final goal, I thought, was the destruction of the United Nations if he could not control it.

Leading in some manner at least to this same conclusion was the explanation given by Khrushchev and by other Soviet representatives of why they wanted to put the troika into effect rather than have a single, independent Secretary General. They gave these reasons with almost appalling candor.

They said that they wanted to arrange matters in such a way that the Secretariat of the United Nations could never do anything that the Soviet Union did not want it to do, in spite of what the General Assembly vote might have been regarding that purpose. Therefore, we heard Khrushchev stating loudly before the entire General Assembly, which at that time consisted of an even hundred members, "Even if the vote were ninety-nine to one against the Soviet Union," he said, "the Soviet Union will have no part of anything which we do not approve." As long as the Secretariat could be operated by three persons, each representing one of the major power blocs of the world, or at least one of the three so-called ideologies, we could be sure nothing would be done of which the Soviet Union disapproved. Apparently, of course, he either ignored or did not care about the fact that this could work both ways —that a representative of one of the other ideologies might be successful in blocking action on something that the Soviet Union wanted very much and in fact had even secured a majority for in the United Nations. Be that as it may, almost all students of international administration, as well as of business or government anywhere, are well agreed that a troika of administration as suggested by the Soviet Union simply could not work. The fact that the Soviets got so little support for it in the General Assembly is, of course, the basic reason why they dropped the idea, at least temporarily. But it is my belief that they will keep trying in other organizations and keep trying for some time yet to come.

As history will attest, during that 1960 Assembly session, Khrushchev indulged in many activities in addition to his well-publicized shoe-pounding. There were his public embraces of Fidel Castro, his Juliet-like appearances on the balcony of the Soviet Mission building, and many other such didos. Having beaten him 70 to 0 on the Congo in the Assembly and called two points of order on him for unseemly language about President Eisenhower during the turbulent debates, I could not expect to be considered one of his favorite people. In fact, when asked about disarmament by some newsmen, he at one point drew out a pocket knife, waved it about with the statement that it was his only weapon, and suggested it could be used to "slit that sack, Wadsworth."

Two days later, at an official Soviet reception, he greeted me like a long-lost brother, and tried to give me a bear hug like the one he had bestowed on Dag Hammarskjöld, just ahead of me in line. The hug was avoided, but Khrushchev, with unquenchable high spirits, called attention to my outsize bulk with the remark: "There's a real American for you!"

Among the speakers who had to cope with Khrushchev's antics in the Assembly chamber, it was British Prime Minister Harold Macmillan who won top honors. About halfway through Macmillan's speech, Khrushchev bounded to his feet and called out loudly in Russian. Macmillan lifted one eyebrow at this gross violation of custom (nobody had ever heckled from the Assembly floor before), and continued his statement. Thereupon Khrushchev shouted again, even louder. It was later established by a United Nations interpreter that he was not calling a point of order, but trying to rebut Macmillan's arguments. Macmillan, unable to understand what was being shouted, calmly turned to the Assembly President, Ireland's Frederick H. Boland, and suggested that if the Leader of the U.S.S.R. wished to make a speech, it would be better for him to make it from the rostrum so that interpreters could relay it to the Assembly. Amid much applause for this suggestion, Khrushchev resumed his seat, chagrined at his failure to throw the Assembly into confusion.

At a luncheon that day given by the Foreign Minister of Australia, R. G. Casey, for the departing Macmillan, I found myself sitting beside the guest of honor, who was his usual "unflappable" self. I mentioned the morning's heckling incident—in fact, it was the chief topic of conversation at the lunch. When the Prime Minister rose to respond to the toast of farewell, he said that he really couldn't see that there was anything to make a fuss about. Anyone brought up in the British political game, he observed, not only became accustomed to biting personal heckling, he was actually somewhat disconcerted when allowed to complete a statement without being interrupted at least once!

The behavior of Khrushchev and other Soviets at the U.N. does not really indicate whether they wish to rule or ruin the organization. Subsequent events tended to show that although he wanted desperately to control, Khrushchev could be expected to rein in short of the destruction point. In the fall of 1962, the Seventeenth General Assembly won through to at least a temporary acceptance of the single Secretary General for the balance of the unexpired term, rather than the three-headed monster desired by the Soviets. I have noted the lack of support in the General Assembly for this idea. In fact, my information is that there was only lukewarm support for the troika within the East European Communist bloc. It is all very well to oppose, and try to change, certain things in major international organizations. In fact, the strategy of "agin-ism" has been more successful than it needed to be over the past sixteen years, but to press deliberately on a course which might have destroyed the whole complex—that is another matter entirely. As long as the organization remains in existence, there is always hope for some extent of control if some of the other campaigns should succeed or if other countries should change their minds; but, if the organization is choked out of existence by Soviet-inspired and Soviet-backed policies, then nothing is left to control, and who gets all the blame?

The student of the United Nations must understand these forces swirling throughout all the streams of the organization. He should not be expected to approve fully all these decisions, no matter where his sympathies may lie. To understand this Glass House, you must try to see it as all others see it, and that means you must look at it from many different standpoints, representing every important nationalist, ideological, and geographical point in the spectrum. It is all very well to dismiss the position of this or that member or group as unrealistic or shortsighted or even "completely unacceptable." If we are to achieve reasonable understanding, which alone can lead to success, then we must at least hold in abeyance the occasional natural inclination to reject out of hand that which we cannot fully embrace.

So, for one obvious example, let us examine the Soviet Union position vis-à-vis the Glass House. First, consider that the U.S.S.R. is conceded to be one of the two most powerful nations in the world, that she has huge military, natural, and intellectual resources, that she is proud and jealous and suspicious of her competitors. Next, consider that she is motivated by an ideology that is traditionally ruthless, that Marxist-Leninist doctrine believes itself superior to any other "ism," that struggle is the key word in her lexicon, and that world domination by international Communism is her long-established goal. Third, consider that the United Nations organization, of which the Soviet Union is a founding member, has almost without exception followed the lead of the United States and her allies. Over and over, it has rebuffed Soviet ideas and proposals and has scorned their complaints. It has buried them with monotonous regularity as a pitifully small minority under an avalanche of United Nations votes, even on issues where Soviet influence might have been thought to be strong. Put only these things in the light of the assumption that they believe they are right and then consider what your own attitude would be under the circumstance. Note that I do not say that they *are* in the right and should, therefore, feel aggrieved. I say, they *believe* they are right and that as a consequence we should not be surprised at their attitude of grievance.

As another example, take the attitude of the United Kingdom. Here is a nation with long and glorious traditions, of great organizing abilities, of courage and a high degree of sophistication in international relations. Here is a power that has seen her status grow from a small island kingdom to the greatest empire in the world. What is even more important, here is a great colonial power that has steadily worked for many years to bring her colonies to independence with a minimum of bloodshed and difficulty—a colonial power that has deliberately shed her executive direction over hundreds of millions of people.

Here is a nation with great pride in her history, both in the stage of exploration, colonization, and conquest, and in the stage of peaceful dissolution into the Commonwealth system. We of the New World will never fully appreciate the travail the United Kingdom went through to achieve her present position. We will never know the intense struggles, internal and external, that took place during this amazing transition. Yet the United Kingdom is subject to ceaseless and violent attack in the United Nations for having been a colonial power, with never a word of credit from her detractors for the magnificent job done. Her "colonies" are precious few and far between these days, and all of them scheduled for independence in the near future. But to the Communist bloc, the British are still "the Colonizers," and to many of the Asians and Africans, they are still the hated former rulers. To others not directly concerned with the colonial issue, they seem to be more or less respectable but somewhat beyond the pale because of friendships and alliances with those who might not command respect.

What probably hurts the most is that the U.K. is no longer the great world power she used to be, and in the United Nations she is sometimes treated accordingly. I realize with some apprehension that when former Secretary of State Dean Acheson spoke late in 1962 along this line, he ran into a perfect hurricane of hate on the part of the British. At the same time, I have heard many intelligent and patriotic United Kingdom people volunteer the same sort of opinion, and I expect that it will eventually become tolerable to face the unpleasant fact.

Add these things up, and we can understand why the United Kingdom is apt to feel less than happy with a rambunctious United Nations General Assembly that occasionally rides roughshod over her sensibilities. Her sense of fair play is often badly bruised by the welcome and consideration accorded to the Soviet Union by certain Afro-Asian members, who determinedly refuse to look at the Communist colonial system while they belabor the country that has freed them and so many others. As a British diplomat once said to me: "This is the worst case of a double standard of political morality in modern history."

What we of the United States, as well as the United Kingdom, do not understand, or at least do not recognize fully, is that the governments and representatives of former colonies, all of which belong to nonwhite races, look at this from a purely racial point of view. A very highly placed Indian once told me: "You simply have to recognize that in India, most of the people cannot get excited over a 'rape of Hungary' or the enslavement of East European peoples. Their concept of 'colonialism' is limited strictly to white domination over nonwhite, and they could not care less what whites do to other whites."

"By the same token," I asked, "what about nonwhites against nonwhites?"

"This is equally outside 'colonialism,'" he replied. "There may be aggression, inhuman treatment, invasion of the sacred homeland as in the Sino-Indian border troubles, but not 'colonialism.' Even the Red Chinese takeover of Tibet is not 'colonialism,' whereas the Indian liberation of the Portuguese enclaves was the strongest of anticolonial moves, since it freed nonwhites from the rule of whites. It will take at least two generations to change this feeling."

And so it is in the United Nations, at least up to a point.

When a resolution calls for an end to colonialism, it is impossible for the representative of a former colony to oppose it, even though the provisions of the resolution are absurd. The Soviet Union, purely as a mischief-making proposition, has several times introduced measures calling for an end to all colonialism within the year. Not only does she have no intention of freeing her own captives in Eastern Europe, but she knows that several United Nations members have carefully and painstakingly negotiated independence accords with their remaining colonies for specified agreed dates. These members know only too well what can happen if independence comes too soon, as it did in the Belgian Congo, and they want desperately to prepare their wards for self-government through careful training and education. Other members have recently emerged into independence, and they, too, know the pitfalls of premature release. Yet, in the main, even these bad resolutions pass by solid majorities, unless an acceptable one can be put to the vote first.

Other typical examples include the Arab League. A large part of its international position is colored, sometimes violently, by hatred of the State of Israel. Arabs will be a long time forgiving and probably never will forget that the United Nations brought this state into being, made her a member of the world body, and has watched over her well-being with the anxious care of a responsible foster mother. To the Arabs, with few exceptions, Israel is an upstart nation that gained her stature and land in Palestine by naked aggression, and that must eventually be "driven into the sea." The Arab Palestine refugees, now nearly a million strong, sit in their camps just over the Israeli border and are rehearsed in their hatred every day.

To one coming, as I did, to view this situation in the United Nations without prior knowledge or prejudice, the Palestine question is the most tragic of all the perennial challenges faced by the international community. I have talked at great length with Arab and Israeli diplomats, and I see no light at the end of the tunnel so long as the sickness of hate grips them both. The Israelis, to be sure, have consistently declared themselves ready to sit at a peace table; the Arabs as consistently have refused. The Arabs have constantly called for repatriation and remuneration for the refugees who fled from their homes before advancing Israeli forces in 1947–48; the Israelis show no inclination to admit strongly hostile people into their territory, although they have declared themselves willing to discuss remuneration, and relocation of the refugees among Arab states willing to receive them. The Arabs will not admit readiness to receive refugees, even in areas where labor is in short supply, because this would be contrary to their position that the refugees must be repatriated and must not be settled elsewhere.

After listening to the violent speeches and arguments on both sides for eight years, I am still loath to take any position as to who is right and who is wrong. All through my service at the United Nations, I tried to take a pro-United Nations position in calling for the settlement of quarrels by peaceful means. You can thus find in the record of both the Security Council and the General Assembly statements by me deploring and condemning, now a series of Arab raids on Israeli farm kibbutzim, now an Israeli military retaliation against such raids. The net result of this, I must ruefully admit, was that the Israeli delegation condemned me as pro-Arab, and the Arabs considered me pro-Israeli! I suppose that they should not be blamed since they were judging, alternately, by what I said on the record. Yet I was neither then and am neither now.

Outside of purely Israeli items, the Arab League members pay, of course, strict attention to the interests of their geographic and ethnic group. They are not monolithic as a bloc, and President Nasser of the United Arab Republic has so far been unsuccessful in organizing a Pan-Arab movement to bring all the various states into a reasonably tight organization. This is not surprising, since the traditions and troubles of the

Middle East are not so easily surmountable. In common with other blocs and organizations, there is a decided divergence of views both political and international. Morocco, Jordan, and Saudi Arabia are still hereditary monarchies; Lebanon, Syria, Tunisia, and Yemen now are classed as republics along with Egypt and the Sudan. Algeria has gained independence but has not yet shown the exact form of government with which it can be labeled. Sudan and Kuwait are members of the bloc, but Mauritania is not.

The Latin American bloc, boasting the oldest multilateral organization, the Organization of American States, comes closer to true cooperation on a voluntary basis than most groups. With nearly total similarity in language, religion, and ethnic background, it has been able to accept Brazil (Portuguese in background) and Haiti (French in background) without too much difficulty. At this writing, Cuba is the only original Organization of American States member in formally poor standing, with all but one of the L.A.'s (as they are called in the United Nations) having withdrawn diplomatic recognition as a result of the leadership of the Castros. Even so, there are still more perennial sore spots than reach the daily headlines.

In Central America, there has been more or less constant friction, with Costa Rica, Guatemala, Honduras, and Nicaragua indulging in various spats among themselves and all of them quarreling to some extent with the Dominican Republic of Rafael Trujillo and the Cuba of Fidel Castro. Panama until recently seems to have saved most of its spleen for the United States over the Canal situation, while sporadic arguments break out in South America among the governments of Argentina, Paraguay, Peru, Chile, and Ecuador.

Few, if any, of these matters come to the United Nations for discussion, much less decision. By dint of long usage, if Latin American governments cannot agree as a result of bilateral talks, the Organization of American States can nearly always arrive at an answer that can be accepted. When the Dominican crisis erupted in April, 1965, the U.N. was brought into the dispute while the OAS was still actively engaged in negotiations. The introduction of the U.N. in a matter involving the OAS is the exception rather than the rule, however. In general, the Latin American countries present a front of unusual unity on international issues, and can be counted on to adhere to well-tried principles in all their dealings.

Some say that the Latin Americans are overlegalistic at times, and it is true that many hours of debate are spent resolving small legalistic differences of opinion. It is also true that Latin American oratory tends to be somewhat more lengthy than our matter-of-fact approach. Despite the impatience delegates may occasionally feel when exposed to such oratory, Peru's Víctor Belaúnde, a superb practitioner of this art, is one of the best-loved delegates ever to come to the U.N., and he richly deserves all the affection lavished upon him. He is wise, strong, moderate—with vast experience in United Nations matters as an "original founder" in San Francisco in 1945. As the acknowledged Demosthenes of the U.N., he exhibits a free-swinging style of oratory, somewhat florid but never pompous. His gestures are magnificent, his voice control masterly. He occasionally has a text or notes before him, but rarely seems to consult them.

On one occasion, so the story goes, Dr. Belaúnde, having completed a particularly resounding presentation, dropped a piece of paper as he strode back to his seat in the General Assembly chamber. Another delegate, picking up the paper, saw that it was part of a prepared text, with a marginal note in Dr. Belaúnde's handwriting. It said simply: "Weak point here. *Shout.*" And, I hasten to repeat, so the story goes.

Despite the time consumed because of the rhetorical and legalistic propensities of the Latin Americans, we enjoy the former, and as adherents of a government of law rather than of men, we should have no quarrel with the latter. We are glad that the overwhelming majority of these governments agree with the free world on the burning issues of the day, and that the stabilizing influence of those twenty solid votes has so often been cast on our side.

This does not mean that all Latin American countries always vote with the United States on all issues. Far from it, and often for good and sufficient reason. But we can say that through the years of its existence, the United Nations has had little need to fear disruptive challenges from this part of the world. Guatemala's Communist regime raised some difficulty in 1953–54, and of course Cuba has been a running sore since Castro's emergence as an avowed Marxist-Leninist. It is still my belief and trust that the Organization of American States will eventually clean up this family quarrel and relieve the United Nations from further worry about it.

The case of the Indian-Pakistani quarrel over Kashmir is one of the oldest in point of years—it has plagued both countries and the Security Council of the United Nations since 1948. Here again one runs into an adamant position on both sides. Once again we find it to be another family-type quarrel, where a large percentage of the leaders of both nations grew up together, played together, went to school and college together, and even fought shoulder to shoulder during two world wars. As in the case of Palestine, the rights and wrongs of it do not seem as important to me today as the peaceful resolution of it. Perhaps if Pakistan would admit a certain amount of responsibility for having moved troops into the Kashmir, and India would admit that a large percentage of the Kashmiri are Moslem and therefore eligible, under original partition ideas, to belong to Pakistan—ah well! Wishful thinking, I fear; and even then no guarantee of helpfulness under existing conditions of mutual distrust.

As far as U.N. action is concerned, virtually everything that could be done has been done. Resolution after resolution has been passed and speech after speech urging negotiation has been made. Beyond this, the Security Council appointed a United Nations Representative on the subject, the Honorable Frank Graham of the United States, who made trip after trip to both countries, spent hundreds of hours persuading, arguing, suggesting face-saving compromises—all to no avail as far as definitive results are concerned. Talks were started over and over again, and then abandoned.

It was hoped that the Communist Chinese attack on India might cause these two warring siblings to form a common front, but no—Pakistan reported that she was negotiating successfully with the Peking regime over the Sino-Pakistan borders; India was slow to remove troops from the Pakistan border area; Pakistan became infuriated with United States and United Kingdom military aid to India on the ground that it could be used against Pakistan—and so on and on and on. The talks started at the United States–United Kingdom initiative in the winter of 1962–63 have produced nothing of value, and in early stages were barely kept alive at our insistence. Here, as in virtually every difficulty experienced in, around, and by the United Nations, that barrier of jealous insistence on prerogative, that hypersovereignty, that selfishness of which I spoke at the outset of these observations, blocks the way to a settlement so obviously necessary to both parties that one would scarcely think it worthwhile mentioning.

On the one hand, Pakistan, once strongly anti-Communist and apparently thoroughly oriented toward the West and particularly toward the United Kingdom and the United States, and an active member of CENTO, nevertheless seems to be unperturbed by the burgeoning aggression of Communist China in the subcontinent. Yet, if India should fall, Pakistan, particularly the eastern segment, is a sitting duck. For one thing, she has additional troubles with her neighbor Afghanistan, which in turn borders on the Soviet Union.

We cannot, of course, absolve India from all blame in the conflict—Pakistan would not have taken such extreme positions without provocation, at least sufficient to her. The fact is that many days after the danger to India became apparent from the Chinese aggression, a large segment of the best-trained Indian troops were still sitting on the cease-fire line in Kashmir, facing a then nonexistent Pakistani attack. As long as they were there, they represented a threat to the Pakistani, even though it is hard to visualize India being capable of mounting an attack in Kashmir at the same time that she was being routed by the Communist Chinese in the north. But logic and reason do not count in these affairs, either in the United Nations or out in the field. Suspicion, distrust, and hate—these are, unfortunately, the factors that count the most.

And so, in evaluating the challenges to the United Nations and the performance of the United Nations in meeting them, we must give a great deal of weight and time to the inability of individuals, communities, states, national governments, and regional organizations to avoid the numbing consequences of the sickness of hate. It is quite evident that people who hate cannot think clearly—it seems at times as though they cannot think at all. Just as neighbor can hate neighbor, so states can hate states, governments and whole peoples can hate other governments and peoples. The spirit of belligerence and all it can mean erects barrier after barrier to the success of all society, from the individual to the United Nations.

This spirit of belligerence arises in large measure from the conviction of right and wrong, in every sense of those two words. When you think you are right, you feel that you have the right to take certain attitudes and actions against those you believe are wrong. One of the troubles is that you can become so convinced of your eternal rightness that anyone who disagrees or who even tries to mediate your quarrel becomes classified as "wrong." Only too often the United Nations has been so classified, and usually without the slightest justification. "Wrongness," like "rightness," is usually a relative thing. The person, state, or nation that you consider wrong most probably considers himself or itself in the right. Certainly the United Nations does, and it represents the consensus of a great many different governments and peoples. "But that does not make it automatically right!" you exclaim.

"No," I must answer, "it doesn't. But the fact that you are convinced of your rightness to the extent of belligerence doesn't automatically make you right either."

From this sort of conflict come the ills of the world, and the only device that man has evolved to deal with it is the voluntary association, like the United Nations. I am not sorry for the United Nations because men continually challenge it —that, in part, is what it is there for. It can serve as a buffer, as a whipping boy, even as a hated symbol at times, if it must. But it is there, and as I have said earlier, it is still true that everybody wants to join and practically nobody wants to quit. Can you think of a better advertising slogan for a voluntary organization?

5 · On or Off the Agenda

W HILE MANY OF THE U.N.'s decisions are challenged, still other issues never get on the agenda; while a great many crises are brought to the Glass House for action, a good many others seem to dance about just outside the threshold, peeking in, and still others (of considerable importance) stay around the corner or across the street, or in some cases in another part of town entirely. One may also wonder about the standards of morality or courage in the United Nations. At times the members have taken a strong stand and at other times have been almost wishy-washy. There seems to be no particular pattern for this, nothing we could automatically recognize.

For instance, one might say that if a crisis should arise between member nations, it would be handled within the framework of the United Nations, whereas if one or more of the disputants were not members, it would remain outside. Thus we can understand that India and Pakistan would argue about Kashmir inside the organization, and that attempts are made by the organization itself to settle the quarrel. On the other hand, the dispute between the Netherlands and Indonesia over West New Guinea started out and went on for some years as a regular inside item; then went into virtually outside negotiations for settlement.

The long-lasting situation in Southeast Asia and in par-

ticular French Indochina remained almost continuously outside the House. Although the United Nations encouraged
talks both tacitly and openly, there was little if any direct
connection. The conferences were held largely in the Palais
des Nations at Geneva, and reports of progress or lack of it
were made known to United Nations members, but the agreements reached and commissions appointed were the responsibilities of the conference, not the United Nations.

If we are to assume (and we don't) that this one stayed
outside mainly because of the nonmembership of Vietnam,
then we might wonder why the Korean crisis was always
inside. Here the two Koreas and Communist China were involved, none of them members.

Of all the well-recognized crises that have stayed out of the
United Nations, the Berlin situation is perhaps the best known
and the most important. It contains a nonmembership factor
in that neither segment of Germany belongs to the Glass
House, but it also carries very unusual consideration because
of the firsthand interest of NATO and the Warsaw Pact
countries. It is in the very heart of the geographic area that
has spawned both of the two world wars, and yet neither
side has shown much desire to have the United Nations take
it over. This in spite of the opening words of the United Nations Charter that refer to the saving of "future generations
from the scourge of war."

I could, I suppose, devote a large amount of space to a series
of arguments, pro and con, on the merits of these various
disputes, situations, and dangers to the peace. It may be of
more value, however, if I try to trace the underlying reasons
why some items have never become full-fledged Glass House
projects to be studied, debated, and solved, also why some
have inspired tough action and some not so tough. I should
stress again that in making these analyses, I am advancing
opinions that are strictly my own and that may be, in some

cases, diametrically opposed to the ideas of the State Department or other parts of the United States Government.

First, a few general rather than specific comments. I have said that the main stumbling block to international cooperation and understanding is the factor of selfish sovereignty that pervades all international relations and particularly those relations which are multilateral in nature. This was the reason underlying the writing of Article 2, Chapter 7, of the United Nations Charter—the chapter that makes it clear that neither the United Nations nor any other nation is supposed to interfere with the internal operations or policies of any member state.

It is a foregone conclusion that had this provision been omitted from the Charter, literally dozens of prospective members in 1945 would have balked at ratification—certainly the United States would have been among them. The stretching of this concept out of all semblance to the original is dealt with in the preceding chapter and need not occupy our attention at this juncture. We must always keep in mind, however, that no matter how much you stretch it and for whatever reason, the desire *not to be interfered with* has neither diminished nor disappeared, and it is still foremost among the factors that guide foreign policy all over the world.

When we come to apply this universal desire, or conceit, or whatever you want to call it, to the questions of whether a quarrel should be taken to the United Nations and how it should be handled there, there are an infinite variety of reactions. To mention the more common of them:

A dispute may be taken to the United Nations because a member nations feels itself aggrieved or victimized by another member nation, and wishes relief and redress for itself as well as a scolding for its persecutor. This is the classic recourse of small and weaker nations, and has been used perhaps more than any other. It stems from the desire for survival and is the most potent reason for joining the Glass House.

The same type of dispute may be kept out of the United Nations because the aggrieved nation believes its persecutor to be too influential or to be the friend of a too influential member so that the complaint will get nowhere. In these cases, the aggrieved may form or join alliances or call upon more powerful friends to help him out. This fatalism is not too common, but the hesitation about utilizing the United Nations in complaints against leaders in the Cold War is present, all the same.

A complaint may be lodged purely for purposes of Cold War propaganda or for the utilization of the ever-ready anti-colonialism ploy. It is not really expected to receive earnest consideration, to say nothing of a majority vote. Often it never gets put to the vote. These run from the obvious "cry-baby" type, accusing the big power of threatening imperialistic designs on the little fellow, to the full throated "bull-elk" type, usually proposed by the Soviet Union against the United States in a direct confrontation of charge and countercharge in the Cold War.

Yet propaganda-type quarrels are quite often kept out of the Glass House for any of several reasons. The "plaintiff" may consider that he has a better case for radio and other publicity statements than for United Nations debate. The "defendant" may notify the "plaintiff" that if the matter is brought to New York, a countercharge will be entered concerning which the "plaintiff" is vulnerable. The "defendant" may be able to negotiate for silence in any number of ways more persuasive than threats, ranging all the way down to appeasement or even purchase. These latter cases are extremely rare and impossible to identify.

Some disputes of long standing may occasionally disappear from the agenda of the General Assembly because the plaintiff decides it is not in his interest to continue. The charge may have been dropped; it may have been laughed out of court at several previous sessions; the plaintiff may have simply become tired or bored with it. Occasionally the original plaintiff may have been put on the defense by recent developments. At other times, regrettably few, outside negotiation has so improved the situation that an Assembly debate is deemed unnecessary or even counterproductive.

Sometimes a dispute, although truly serious, is not brought to the Glass House because of the reluctance of the key member states involved. We have already mentioned Berlin in this category. This was also the case in the Indochinese situation in Southeast Asia, where France insisted that these were matters outside the jurisdiction of the United Nations. In spite of the fact that the fighting as well as the politics seemed to spell the end of French control in that area, France refused to ask for help except from her close friends on an individual basis, and that proved too little and too late. When she finally agreed to sit at a conference table to talk about a Southeast Asian Treaty and a Treaty Control Commission, it was, as I said earlier, a conference outside the jurisdiction of the United Nations. It was organized by the United Kingdom and the Union of Soviet Socialist Republics, whose representatives sat at the table as Co-Chairmen of the group. The Control Commission named by the group consisted of Canada for the "West," Poland for the "East," and India for the "neutrals." Parenthetically, the conspicuous lack of success of this Commission should have demonstrated the fallacy of the troika theory, expounded then and still more or less embraced by the Soviet Union. During its checkered career, the Commission has rarely agreed on anything, and I have often wondered whether a good many intelligent Frenchmen have not regretted their government's refusal to use the United Nations forum early in the game. Surely they could not have received any worse treatment at the hands of the full organization than they did from the Southeast Asian Conference at Geneva.

The Korean question started in the Glass House and has remained there ever since, largely because the United States felt that the United Nations had an outstanding opportunity to operate under the terms of the "collective action" provisions of the United Nations Charter. It is important to understand the circumstances under which this sort of action is possible as well as when it is not possible. There has to be a combination of geographical and political factors in such juxtaposition as to persuade the General Assembly or the Security Council or both that the use of armed force in collective action is not only necessary but appropriate, and comparatively free from the danger of repercussion against members for having voted it.

Korea met most of the tests for propriety and reality. It was fairly accessible geographically; personnel and supplies could be moved there without violating national boundaries of friend, foe, or neutral. The aggression was initiated by the Communist regime of North Korea, ironically carrying the title of "People's Republic," a nonmember of the Glass House without much international standing, and with few friends except in Communist circles. The government of the Republic of Korea was not only responsible; it was *there*—in charge of operating the country and its military forces. As long as the fighting was limited to the Korean peninsula, there was no reason for the Kremlin or Peking to try and widen the scope of the war, although there were many who believed that they might have liked to.

And so fifteen nations agreed to join together with the United States and the Republic of Korea to save the latter from Communist engulfment. In addition to the fifteen combatants, some of the "neutral" nations, notably India and Sweden, provided aid in the form of hospital ships, field hospitals, and hospital teams, and a considerable quantity of medical and surgical equipment and supplies.

Thus the Korean incident provided the first known collective military operation in the history of multilateral foreign relations. Since it was the first, there were many bugs to be ironed out, and criticism still crops up from time to time over the way the situation was handled.

It is not my purpose to defend policy decisions here, or to join the chorus of critics. I will point out as forcefully as I can that the outcome of the Korean affair was almost exactly what the founders of the United Nations envisaged when they built collective action into the Charter. Naked aggression was stopped and thrown back; the victim of aggression kept her entity and sovereignty intact; the United Nations forces were not used to win total victory or new territory in behalf of anybody; the final agreements were achieved through negotiation. Like it or not, and many Americans do not because it could scarcely be called a "victory," this is what the United Nations is for.

Among the criticisms one hears regularly against the Glass House is that it did nothing to help the Hungarian patriots in their desperate battle for freedom in 1956. What we must recognize is that, just as the Korean incident might be considered to have had the right factors working in favor of collective action, the Hungarian incident had all the wrong ones.

Consider its geographic location: totally inaccessible by land or water without impinging on either neutral Austria or one of the East European Communist states. To have had a military expedition large enough to confront even the comparatively few Soviet troops who were there when Premier Nagy fell, would have taken a fantastic personnel and logistics airlift. Under the terms of the Austrian State Treaty of 1955, that country could not even allow overflight of such an airlift if it wanted to, and that would have meant running the gantlet of antiaircraft fire and fighter planes over neutral and Communist territory.

The aggressive action in Hungary was taken by the leader of the Communist bloc, one of the two strongest military powers in the world, commanding prestige if not affection in all parts of the world, and wielding a mighty legal weapon in the provisions of the Warsaw Pact. This treaty requires the Soviet Union, if called upon, to help any other treaty members against enemies either external or internal. You can be sure that such a call was made, even though it might not have resounded to the four corners of the earth. The Soviets saw to it.

In contrast to Korea, the government of Hungary was virtually nonexistent; it was in Budapest only because the Soviet troops were supporting it. A United Nations collective action, therefore, would have been in support of a rebel regime that could not even pretend to be a government, even in exile, and that had no standing whatever. The Charter makes no provision for, nor can anyone spell out in advance, conditions whereby a group seeking to establish itself as a government can be given assistance against the constituted authorities, although such authorities might not command wide popular support at home.

Finally, although there may have been plenty of room for doubt that the Soviets would risk all-out war over a Korea, a Cuba, or even a Berlin, a Hungary in 1956 was a different thing. This would have been tantamount to war on Soviet territory, and expanding the scope of a war that would come so close to the motherland would be almost a certainty.

All in all, then, there was virtually no chance at all that collective action could have been voted even if the United States had taken a strong position for it. As a matter of fact, we were told quite plainly that there would be almost no support for such a move, and our nose count bore this out. And that is why the General Assembly of the United Nations perforce contented itself with "calling upon" the Soviet Union and its puppet Hungarian Government to stop their repressive activities. The Assembly also appointed first a committee and then a representative to keep in touch with the situation. Not a record to be vastly proud of, particularly since we all knew that the Soviets and their puppets would thumb their noses at the Assembly, its committee, and its representatives. I believe the committee once got as far as Vienna and interviewed some Hungarian refugees. Neither it nor either of the representatives, both former Presidents of the General Assembly (Prince Wan of Thailand and Sir Leslie Munro of New Zealand), ever set foot on Hungarian soil. Secretary General U Thant made a visit but not until July of 1964, when the matter had pretty well died down.

But, though the record may be sorry, one has to consider the alternatives, and there was no doubt that a collective action or even a unilateral action on our part would have been costly to a ghastly degree. It would have meant going up against the strongest conventional military establishment of the time, virtually on its own grounds, with our own lines of supply dependent on an airlift, with all the dangers that implies. It would have been a difficult enough job if one had been able to guarantee the success of the enterprise; no one even pretended that such a guarantee could be made. Therefore the alternative to what was done was undoubtedly war of considerable proportions, very possibly world-wide and probably eventually nuclear in character. *The United Nations is not in the business of starting such wars.*

Of all the puzzling paradoxes that beset the student of the Glass House, the ever-present one of disarmament probably takes first rank. This is an issue that has oscillated between a place on the agenda and a site "out" of the Glass House.

In the beginning, it was strictly "in," with a twelve-member Disarmament Commission composed of the eleven members of the Security Council, plus Canada. In 1955 a subcommittee of that group was officially formed and blessed, consisting of the "major powers": France, the U.K., the U.S., the U.S.S.R., and again, Canada.

In 1957 the smaller nations, including most of the non-aligned group, became discouraged with the lack of progress of the big powers and bid for more influence on the subject. The result of this was unfortunate and even somewhat ludicrous, since no agreement could be reached on how many additional members should serve on the Disarmament Commission. Even if a figure might have been agreed upon, the identity of the new members was politically impossible to negotiate because everybody either wanted to get into the act or felt that as a matter of prestige they had to get into the act.

So, the new Disarmament Commission of the General Assembly was formed, with a membership of the entire General Assembly! Obviously a group so large would be far too unwieldy for negotiating purposes; the few times it has met it has floundered in a sticky mess of propaganda speeches and has accomplished nothing but a series of appeals to the major powers to come to agreement. Each year, the Political Committee of the General Assembly listens to a long series of self-seeking, self-serving speeches on the part of East and West alike. Each year, they hear words that sound as though the areas of agreement were growing in scope and depth. Each year, they hopefully applaud the ephemeral and gently tut-tut the tangible.

Yet this is quite understandable, in fact. If you take the factors of sovereignty and selfishness, and mix them thoroughly with suspicion, fear, and the creeping sickness of hate, you get what I call the security stew, in which too much of the world sits and simmers. It is no wonder that the nations of the world, mired in this viscous mess, have not been able to find the answer to this most pressing of all subjects.

From time to time, the various powers tentatively stretch a toe toward the waters outside the Glass House, to see whether initiatives could not be discovered that might open the way to more meaningful discussions. The outstanding examples of this had little to do with the main current of disarmament, but they were perhaps tributary streams that were well worth exploring. The first, an Eisenhower project, started in December, 1954, and concluded successfully in 1956, was the formation of the International Atomic Energy Agency, which began a series of talks among the atomic nations of the West and ended up in an eighty-two-nation ratifying conference in the Glass House. The second, also an Eisenhower project, started in the spring of 1958 and developed late that fall into the Conference on a Nuclear Weapons Test Ban Treaty. After many ups and downs, mostly the latter, a limited treaty was agreed upon and signed in early 1963, banning tests in the atmosphere, underwater, and in outer space, but not affecting underground explosions. This conference, originally visualized as one among nuclear powers only, is not only outside the United Nations but, because of France's refusal to join it, does not even represent all the nuclear powers. The three powers who originally signed the limited treaty are now acting somewhat as a subcommittee of the United Nations Seventeen-Nation Committee on Disarmament, but it is still outside the United Nations, since it can and does arrive at decisions without regard to the Seventeen-Nation group or the United Nations itself. And in spite of the signing of the limited treaty, the major premise remains that of the security stew.

Having been actively concerned with the negotiations on disarmament since 1953, and with considerable responsibility since 1955, I have lost all sense of wonder over the failure of mankind to agree to disarm. In common with most of the diplomats and politicians who have struggled with the problem, I have been annoyed, disappointed, frustrated, enraged, disgusted. But I hope that I have been able to achieve a perspective; that I have been able to rise above mire, mist, and miasma to view the tangled scene as dispassionately as most.

The security stew is no nation's exclusive recipe. All of us contribute the various ingredients, and each of us is occasionally prone to stir it with the spoon of our own national security, occasionally to spice it with our own brand of peppery nationalism.

Let me assure you that there is nothing to be overly proud of in our handling of the disarmament issue. In the face of the Communist threat, there has been every reason for being prudent and at least keeping our powder dry, but Americans have made such a fetish of strength and deterrence that the security stew has managed to dull our taste buds.

Since the earliest days of "Don't tread on me," the American people have been prone, under provocation, to bristle into a belligerence quite startling in contrast to our normal easygoing amiability. One of the difficulties is that it is hard to predict just what sort of provocation is apt to trigger off this reaction. In recent history, we can mark the Cuban situation of the fall of 1962. Yet there have been times when we have kept our equanimity comparatively well when faced with threat or action. Usually such incidents are a long way from our shores and therefore loom less large in our consciousness.

But the same reactions that make the people of the United States see red—in more ways than one—make the government of the United States hypercautious in dealing on disarmament with the Soviet Union. As everybody knows only too well, there simply is not enough trust in today's world to make a successful negotiation out of Geneva. The Soviets distrust us as much as we distrust them, though not, we think, with such reason. This is why our negotiators go round and round in a scarcely graceful minuet at Geneva and elsewhere. This is why our official policy positions invariably strive to guarantee a better military capability than that of the "other side" throughout the stages of every disarmament plan of the past fifteen years.

I am not trying to claim that every position taken by our government is *wrong;* that is a word whose meaning is almost as difficult to pin down as the meaning of the word "right." There have been times, and there will certainly continue to be times, when "enlightened self-interest" will impel us to take positions that *seem* wise in the light of potential danger to our security. But whether enlightened or not, the fact remains that it *is* self-interest, and it is this concept, whether "right" or not, that keeps us from making progress in disarmament.

Although the McCloy-Zorin agreement of September, 1961, revealed what was apparently a wide area of agreement in principle, this has not been borne out in negotiation of details. For example, one of the key agreements in that document, paragraph 5, reads as follows: "All measures of general and complete disarmament should be balanced so that at no stage of the implementation of the treaty could any state or group of states gain military advantage, and that security is ensured equally for all." Yet in the negotiations subsequent to the signing of that agreement, both the United States and the Union of Soviet Socialist Republics have held basically to positions which would at least *keep* if not *gain* military advantage; positions which have been denounced and rejected by the "other side" for precisely that reason, and are thus not negotiable.

How can this process be called negotiation? Of course, it is not negotiation and is scarcely meant to be. Both sides make a great point of wanting to negotiate; both sides proclaim themselves flexible and ready to compromise; neither side believes the other for one moment. It is a tragic sort of minuet we are dancing, because both sides know perfectly well that they are flirting with complete annihilation by not checking and turning back the wildly spiraling arms race. The tragedy lies not so much in the *fact* of potential annihilation as in the *knowledge* of it, because that knowledge, until recently, has been accompanied daily by word and deed that deny it.

Why? Such a simple word, and so very hard to answer. The simplest way of answering is the hardest to understand. It is that neither the major powers nor a good many of the middle- and smaller-sized powers are ready to take what they fear to be the risks of disarmament. They are not ready to trust their potential adversaries or the rest of the world to the extent necessary to achieve a treaty that all can live with. This simplest answer is not difficult to understand in terms of the words involved—those are blunt and clear enough. What is difficult for me to grasp is that those beliefs should be held and those distrusts should be so paramount as to make the blunt words true, in these days of the nuclear weapon.

Which holds the greater set of risks: disarmament, or the arms race? Every important world figure, except the ruling figures of Chinese and Albanian Communism, tells us that the arms race is vastly more risky than disarmament. Are we to believe that they themselves are lying when they say that? Are we to believe that our government, as well as all the other enlightened governments of the world, is really secretly hoping for an all-out nuclear war? That is what we accuse each other around the world of wanting, or, at the very least, "military warmongering imperialism" and "international Communist conspiracy."

One more thought before we leave the subject of disarmament in and out of the Glass House, and that concerns the role and position of the smaller powers in the whole business. People are inclined to accept the thesis that the sole responsibility for the achievement of disarmament resides in the major powers, specifically the United States and the Union of Soviet Socialist Republics. This is true, to the extent that a disarmament treaty cannot be concluded unless the major powers agree to it, and to the extent that a disarmament operation cannot succeed unless the major powers live up to it and support whatever action is needed in the United Nations to enforce it.

Yet there is a definite and most important role for smaller member states and all nonmember states to play, the main qualification for which is that they truly and seriously want disarmament for themselves. They live in the Glass House, and only too often are inclined to throw stones at the great powers for not having come to agreement about arms. Yet virtually none of them has ever done anything constructive about the matter themselves. There is, I am told, only one member state in the whole United Nations which can claim that it has no army, navy, or air force: Costa Rica. The rest have spent desperately needed resources to support military establishments of various sizes. Sometimes, we find, the military forces have scarcely been used, even internally, for the last quarter of a century.

Then there is the group of potentially strong powers which have insisted on keeping their neutrality or "nonalignment" in the Cold War, and which have regularly called for peace and disarmament in the world. This group includes India, Indonesia, and the United Arab Republic, among many others. Their chiefs of state have often met and issued ringing statements on the necessity for a world-wide cessation of conflict and a laying down of arms. Yet what is one to believe when India decides to liberate the Portuguese enclaves on her coast by overwhelming military might, and has kept strong forces facing the Pakistani in Kashmir for many years? And what are we to believe when Indonesia pawns her future for Communist arms, first with the announced intention of liberating West New Guinea by force, and then with the threat of crushing the Federation of Malaysia?

What are we to believe when Nasser sends his troops to Yemen and various other parts of the Arab world to subvert established governments and support rebel movements? Regardless of rationalizations about colonialism and tyranny and all the rest, these actions do not bespeak a vast desire for peace; do not demonstrate any desire for disarmament. They are not alone; they are merely used as examples because of recent well-publicized actions. They represent a feeling that is prevalent all over the world about disarmament: "It is a good thing if you can get it; in the meanwhile we will act in accordance with what we deem to be our interests. If these interests call for the use of military force for any purpose whatever, so be it; we will use it. But, of course, disarmament is most desirable, particularly for the great powers!"

Yet in spite of the appalling lack of progress either in or out of the United Nations in regard to disarmament, one must always remember that the best hope of improving the world atmosphere lies not in human nature but in the human institutions which can affect human nature in spite of itself. The United Nations is the outstanding institution in this field, for the reason that it is the only one where world tensions can truly be felt to tighten and relax, without unusual bias being shown.

In the United Nations, very few governments labor under the impression that they are able to pull the wool over all other governments' eyes. Those who try are merely hoping against hope. Therefore, if we can agree that disarmament must *follow* rather than *cause* better feelings between nations great and small, the place to recognize reduction of tension must be at the United Nations. Once reduction of tension is recognized as being backed by some sincerity, the resultant better feeling can move quickly into the disarmament area.

This has been shown quite clearly in the reaction to the "hot line" between the White House and the Kremlin, the limited test ban treaty, and the announcement of cutbacks in the production of weapon-strength nuclear material. People quickly started talking optimistically about other steps that they think may be taken, which, although perhaps not disarmament per se, may still be taken as further evidence of relaxation of Cold War rigidities. Much of the relaxation can be and is inevitably lost when some Communist bigwig excoriates the West in old-time Stalinist terms, or when Peking blares out the accusation that the United States "imperialists" brought about the abortive *coup d'état* in Laos, when the whole world knows that the United States took a strong stand *against* the coup and, almost singlehandedly, caused it to fail.

In the face of these crass dishonesties, it is no wonder that mutually strong appetites for further progress seem to be adversely affected, on the Western side, at least. There is ample cause for nausea! But with all the justifiable and less justifiable indignation continuously expressed by both sides, a strong sense of reality and desire for self-preservation is present in even the more belligerent of the opposing regimes, and we must continue to hope that utter madness will not overtake any of their leaders before they give the great human institution at least a chance to lower the temperature.

6 · Communication

Many people have considered communication difficulties to be limited to language troubles, but this is only a small part of it. Nearly every language in the United Nations has adopted certain phrases that are at least somewhat interchangeable, or that are translated into the various other U.N. languages with a similarity of structure. It is, therefore, not so much a question of translating what the Soviet Representative may say into English—it may be actually a question of what he means when he uses the communal expression.

To an American, words like "liberty," "freedom," "democracy," "human rights," or "peoples" mean certain things, whereas to a Communist, there are strong shades of slanted interpretation in accordance with his ideology. We of the United States are prone to claim proprietorship of many of these much-abused words, since we used them in our fight for independence, and ours was the first such fight of a potential great power. So, when an American visitor to the Glass House first puts on the earphones in the General Assembly or the Security Council, he is apt to be shocked clear to his toenails to hear how the representative of a Communist country is using these hallowed terms.

He is told that what he has always considered one of history's most tightly controlled dictatorships is a "People's

Democratic Government." He hears of the utopian life of "freedom" and "liberty" under such a regime, and how this regime stoutly defends the principles of "peace" and "self-determination" and "coexistence" and "independence" against the vicious attacks of the "imperialist-capitalist-fascist war-mongers" of the United States and of her "decadent," "depraved," "colonizer" friends in Europe and elsewhere.

In this upside-down world, the American listener is assured that only the Soviet Union and her Communist bloc truly desire peace and harmony and "general and complete" disarmament, whereas the United States and her friends are constantly plotting military aggression and blocking disarmament because of their insatiable desire to plunge the world into nuclear war. Every defensive move on our part is labeled aggressive; every aggressive move on their part is labeled purely defensive. The Communist states set up a chant for "disarmament," and at the same time they call for "wars of liberation." They first deny, and then admit, sending offensive weapons to Cuba; then, in perhaps the most brilliant example of inconsistency of the century, claim the laurels of the peacemaker for ceasing to do what they never should have done in the first place!

But Soviets are not alone in the inconsistencies that make communication difficult. The West has indulged in its share, too, and has contributed to the upside-down picture that the Soviet listener sees from his point of view. This is vitally important to understand. The British and French proclaim love of peace just before an armed invasion of Egypt; American Presidents proclaim the imperative need for disarmament at the same time they are asking the Congress for more billions of dollars for arms. The United States Delegate to the United Nations speaks boldly in favor of freedom and independence for all people just before voting against a resolution calling for an end to colonialism. President Kennedy calls for a "peace race," in perhaps the best-received United States speech ever delivered at the United Nations, and within weeks is calling up the reserves to strengthen the Berlin garrison. Israel assumes the pose of broad-minded readiness to make peace but feels impelled to shoot at Arabs regularly.

The United States agrees to "discuss" the Canal treaty with Panama, but refuses to "negotiate" it, this on the ground that the latter word has connotations of appeasement or yielding to pressure. Yet, in the very next breath, we urge the continuance of "negotiations" on disarmament, which have been so devoid of yielding and appeasement for the last seventeen years that no agreement has been possible!

Nor are the so-called nonaligned nations blameless in this modern Tower of Babel. India has stood forth for years as the country that opposes use of military force for any purpose; then comes its action in Goa and, more recently, the Indian-Pakistani war. Indonesia calls, and fronts for, the whole nonaligned world to the Bandung Conference with its famous "Five Points," most of them regularly honored in the breach if at all; then she not only threatens but actually starts an armed invasion of West New Guinea, and later publicly vows to crush the newly independent Federation of Malaysia. Now, when the West New Guinea matter has been concluded by negotiation, and the Malaysia difficulty remains acute, Indonesia is supporting by far the largest military establishment in that part of the world. Why? Thus the tensions roll up in intensity despite the fine phrases.

Clearly, the difficulties in communications I have pointed to are not solely the result of differing cultures, of differing world views between East and West, between "haves" and "have-nots"—although these differences are real and powerful. But the process of communication is used as a weapon, as well, by all nations at one time or another. By wielding this weapon skillfully, they can turn the meaning of a word to their own advantage; "invasion" becomes "liberation" and "dictatorship" becomes "people's democracy." Thus in the field of communications between nations, we again encounter our old antagonist—self-interest.

A historian of the twenty-first century researching the area of international relations in the early 1960's is going to have a field day. Let's hope he has a sense of humor, because if he does not, he may well go mad trying to follow the seeming contradictions of word and deed that whirled around the globe. This may well go down in the history books as the period when a high-minded slogan ran into gales of trouble from all sides, even from the United Nations itself!

The slogan I am talking about is that favorite of the anti-colonialists: "self-determination." Even before the attainment of "complete independence," "full sovereignty" (and, of course, membership in the United Nations), the most jealously guarded right in the book has been that of "self-determination." This is a very easy slogan to learn, and to shout, and perhaps not too difficult to understand, and seemingly so self-explanatory as to require little definition. To give a people the right to determine their own form of government seems to be so logical that any nation adhering to the United Nations Charter could have no hesitation in supporting it.

But all nations, we have learned, have the sovereign right to define "self-determination" as they see fit, and the nuances of meaning are nearly limitless. In addition, there are so many special situations and considerations that any single concept of the phrase is literally impossible. As used in the Glass House, the label has come to have a meaning quite different from that ascribed to it after World War I, where several nationalist groups, notably in the Balkans, insisted on splitting away from countries artificially built by treaty to form more homogeneous states on their own. In the post-World War II days, the great push was for freedom and independence from colonial rule, and the phrase has spread its meaning into a combination of the right to choose one's own rulers and form of government and the right to have a voice in policy decision that may vitally affect the people. Yet, as can be seen, precise agreements and understanding are still impossible.

Let us move about the world of recent years and cover a few of the ways in which governments and leaders have observed the principle of self-determination. In order not to hide behind the actions of others, let us take the Western Hemisphere first, and in particular the United States. Some years ago, we stoutly affirmed the right of the people of Cuba, as exemplified at the time by Fidel Castro, to overthrow the dictatorship of Fulgencio Batista by force. True, many Americans distrusted Castro and pointed to the fact that Batista had been a good friend of the United States, but their voices were drowned in the general acclaim for the revolution. This was self-determination. Were we not ourselves born of revolution and did we not therefore sympathize with all who rose up to crush tyranny?

But little by little, Castro demonstrated his own devotion to the cause of self-determination by clamping down with a Communist police state that turned out to be perhaps even more restrictive than the one he overthrew. Free and open elections were indefinitely postponed, hundreds of "counter-revolutionaries" were dragged to the execution wall, political police prowled everywhere, and the leader indulged in four-, five-, and six-hour radio and television monologues extolling his revolution, denouncing the United States, but failing to deliver any self-determination.

Meanwhile, the United States had become enraged at the hostile words and deeds of the new Cuban dictator, who was waltzing ever closer to the Kremlin although at that time denying it stoutly. So, we decided to display *our* devotion to the cause of self-determination (to say nothing of solemn treaties) by helping the anti-Castro refugees to go back, hoping by force of arms to take over via the Bay of Pigs. Here, a merciful curtain.

The next act was, of course, the great palpitation of October, 1962, resulting in the withdrawal by Khrushchev of certain missiles and the deactivation of certain missile bases. At this writing, it may seem premature to conclude that all offensive weapons and systems have been removed, since no absolute verification can be made. However, this is not our subject. It scarcely needs laboring that neither the placing of the missiles in Cuba by the Soviets, the ultimatum given by President Kennedy, nor their apparent withdrawal by Khrushchev had any relation to self-determination on the part of the Cuban people. We are led to believe, in fact, that the withdrawal was directly contrary to the desire of the Cuban Government, until Castro fortunately discovered that the missiles were not really needed and that the bombers were too old and slow.

An entirely different situation occurred in the case of the Dominican Republic in 1961. We had been aware for a long time that the Dominican people had no chance for self-determination under Generalissimo Trujillo. This well-recognized dictatorship claimed complete propriety on the ground that the people not only needed but wanted "Papa" Trujillo; this, he claimed, added up to self-determination. The people were allowed to vote for the Trujillo-dominated ticket of close Trujillo associates, and this, too, was obviously self-determination!

The United States played this one quite differently. Working with the Organization of American States, we and our closer American friends gradually receded from association with the Dominican regime, until we broke off diplomatic relations with it and applied certain economic sanctions. Soon after the Generalissimo was assassinated, most of his family fled (temporarily), and the government remained in the hands of Trujillo's President Balaguer, backed by the air force and other elements of the military. This did not solve the problems, and the anti-Trujillo people kept up the pressure until a real crisis came along.

We will never know whether the crisis would have erupted into civil war, or whether the military remaining loyal to Balaguer could have overcome other military elements stimulated both ways by the return of several of the Trujillo family. Acting without doubt at the request of the only government of the Dominican Republic, the United States this time showed its devotion to the principle of self-determination by sending warships to patrol off Dominican waters in a quiet but effective demonstration of support for the people in power. That one worked—at least until the next crisis, when we sent in the Marines.

I can hear some of my friends bristling with righteous indignation, ready to point out that in both Cuba and the Dominican Republic there have been circumstances which had to be considered and which militated against any other action. I know this; what I have said about these two cases was not for the purpose of criticizing our own policies and actions. I have tried to show, in just two cases out of many, that the much-touted principle of self-determination is subject to other pressures, other factors and considerations, depending on one's particular viewpoint. If the United States knows that a full-fledged satellite of the Soviet Union is only ninety miles from our shores and that this constitutes a threat to our security, then that should be taken into consideration. If the United States and other American states fear that the return of the Trujillos and civil strife would be bad for one of their sister states, as well as for the whole hemisphere, then that is another consideration that must be weighed. And if later the U.S. believes that a Cuban-inspired Communist takeover is in process, hiding behind a revolution, that is yet another matter.

But let us move to other parts of the world and recall a few more examples of words versus deeds. Also in 1961, Premier Khrushchev, according to the press, decided that Finland was becoming a little too independent. An anti-Soviet candidate for the Finnish Presidency was popular and might have made a good run—he might even have won! So, in accordance with the well-known Soviet principle of self-determination for all peoples who remain loyal to the Kremlin, the President of Finland was called to a conference on the pretext of mutual security in the Baltic against Western Germany. Result: the President of Finland announced that Finland did not have to join a defense movement militarily just yet; the anti-Soviet candidate withdrew from the race; a new version of peace and self-determination on the Baltic emerged.

While we are on the subject of the Soviet Union, the general acquiescence to Soviet-brand protection of Hungary's right of self-determination should not prevent us from noting it. We also note that Albania's espousal of the Peking line may make her eligible for special treatment some day. So far there seems to be charge, countercharge, and worsening of diplomatic relations. If Albania should seem important enough to bring back into the Soviet orbit, there may be more awkwardness than attended the disengagement of Tito's Yugoslavia from the inner circle.

Moving south and west a bit, we find a completely different picture, with President de Gaulle striving for years to give the Algerians a good big dose of self-determination. This, in the face of bitter opposition on the part of many of the French residents of that land: the *colons* and *ultras*, so called. We had the unusual situation of a traditionally colonialist government struggling against a segment of its own people to free a former colony that had been integrated to a large extent into the parent nation. Now that the Algerians have their independence, we will have to wait and see how their self-determination will be utilized. I only hope that they and the rest of the world will never forget the almost incredible job done by President de Gaulle in making all this possible.

Deeply surprising to observers who predicted dire consequences from President Nasser's formation of the United Arab

Republic was the acquiescence with which he greeted Syria's announced desire in 1962 to secede from the Republic and, later, Yemen's decision to withdraw from the Federation of the U.A.R. For whatever reason, President Nasser refused to become excited or to back up his desire for unity with force or even threats of force. He allowed "self-determination" in Syria, first in a nearly bloodless coup and then in the formation of a government apparently acceptable to the people. This question did not enter into the Yemeni decision to withdraw, since their original relationship was that of autonomous states linked in a loose federation. Chalk one up for the classic definition of the slogan! But then, chalk up a different one for Nasser's deliberate intervention on the side of the Yemeni rebels!

Other Arab lands and rulers have been neither acquiescent nor generous about their neighbors' claims to self-determination. When Britain gave Kuwait her independence, President Kassem of Iraq immediately filed his claim to that oil-rich principality. Prompt action by the British under their treaty with Kuwait at least postponed any direct moves leading to Iraq's exercise of her devotion to self-determination by annexation of a weak but very rich neighbor. And in Northwest Africa, Morocco was not merely pained by the decision of Mauritania to become independent. She went so far to prove her support of Mauritanian self-determination that she tried to keep that newborn state out of the United Nations! This attempt, however, finally dissolved in the compromise allowing both Outer Mongolia and Mauritania to become members.

After this compromise was agreed on, I had the opportunity of getting a revealing insight into Soviet attitudes on the matter from Yakob Malik, then a member of the Soviet U.N. Delegation. Malik is probably best remembered as the suave villain who cast scores of Soviet vetoes in the Security Council in 1951 and 1952, but like many other Russian representatives, he was most personable and pleasant when not engaged in actual debate. He headed the Soviet Delegation to the London talks of the Disarmament Subcommittee in 1955 while he was also Ambassador to the United Kingdom, and during that period suffered a heart attack that kept the conference marking time for nearly two weeks.

At the time of the election of Outer Mongolia and Mauritania, he was back in New York at the Security Council. There were a dozen other applicants for membership at this session, most of which had been knocking on the door for several years but had been foiled by Soviet vetoes year after year. The dam was broken when the Soviets acquiesced in the multiple admission of the fourteen, not without great reluctance and stalling to the very end.

After the final unanimous vote, I found myself walking along the hall with Malik, who was looking unusually chipper and happy. Turning to me suddenly, he said: "I don't suppose you will believe it, but this action of the Council fills me with joy. You will never know how it hurt me personally to cast all those vetoes a few years ago. It affected me so strongly each time that I felt sick. I am sure my heart trouble stems directly from this."

One of the bargaining points the U.S.S.R. had raised during the admission discussions had been the admission of Red China in exchange for admission of a Western applicant. But many of the Western delegates found Red China unqualified largely because of her steadfast adherence to her own special definition of the great principle of self-determination. Mao Tse-tung apparently decided that, albeit silently, the Tibetan people had issued an unmistakable call to the Peking regime to rescue them from the Dalai Lama. The fact that the Chinese had to kill a great many Tibetans to rescue them, and that they are still fighting guerrilla actions many years later, is not to the point. The Tibetans, according to Peking, belong to China; they needed and wanted the Communist Chinese to rule them; they got them. Let it also be noted that among the

cries of outrage raised over the Tibetan incident, the Nationalist Chinese were not counted. They, too, consider Tibet as
part of China.

Mao, of course, is most lavish with his largesse of self-
determination. Before the Tibetan rescue he managed to
"liberate" considerable chunks of Burma, and appeared most
astonished that the Burmese Government felt impelled to
object. In addition, he heeded the imperceptible call of the
downtrodden masses along certain sections of the Sino-Indian
border. These territories, traditionally Indian, are, I have
heard it said, among the few places in the world which are so
deserted that large nuclear bombs could be set off without
hurting anybody. Is this why Peking was so anxious to annex
them?

Be that as it may, the Peking invasions and aggressions
against both Burma and India appear to have had at least one
unexpected result. They seem to have helped Prime Minister
Nehru come to a full realization of the enormity, not only of
the Communist Chinese action, but of the 450-year aggression
practiced against India by Portugal, and the deafening cry for
help of the populace of Goa. The Portuguese enclaves on the
west coast of India had been under Portugal's rule since the
early 1500's, and thus there could be no doubt in Delhi that
they represented not only colonialism at its worst, but even a
threat to the security, integrity, and sovereignty of India. One
might as well imagine a huge Bengal tiger becoming concerned over the presence of three small nests of mice on the
edges of his domain. But there were Goa and the others,
"pimples," we are told, on the skin of India. And because they
were there, they festered in Delhi. So they were taken by
overwhelming force. The book may not be closed for some
time on the Sino-Indian border affair that flared briefly into
war during the fall of 1962. Perhaps the Chinese were in turn
emboldened by the success of the Indian action against Goa.

At any rate, we can be sure that our favorite slogan was not involved.

One other thought on the Indian subjugation of the Portuguese enclaves as much through words as through deeds: There is something tragic in the realization that, when the chips were down (and they must have been for reasons still to be demonstrated), Nehru, of all others in the world, would have sent an overwhelming modern military force in aggression against those tiny garrisons. It is still more tragic that at the time his major supporters in world opinion were: the Union of Soviet Socialist Republics, which has not hesitated to threaten or use force when it appears to its interest; Communist China, for which, as Nehru's successors can now attest, the same shoe fits, and Indonesia, which saw in the Indian action the perfect prelude to her own heart's desire.

Once Nehru had shown the way, Sukarno ordered mobilization for the express purpose of invading Dutch New Guinea, which he claimed as part of his island empire as West Irian. How short human memories are, to be sure! By withdrawing from the Glass House, the President of Indonesia has made it plain that he found it useful and easy to forget that if it had not been for the United Nations, with the active prodding of the United States, there would never have been the independent Indonesia that we know today, much less one including West Irian. I am sure that the Dutch have not forgotten. Yet even while negotiations under the auspices of the United Nations were being carried on, and carried on in an atmosphere obviously conducive to settlement, Sukarno actually started hostilities, dropping paratroopers and conducting naval strikes and skirmishes. Thus he demonstrated his devotion to the principles of the United Nations and to our slogan. Self-determination meant to him only that he wanted West Irian. The people of the territory he yearned to liberate contributed only a strident silence in the history of the affair. Since Indonesia received the right to take over West Irian eventually through negotiation, it was somewhat of a triumph for those striving to avert fighting. It may be hailed as a triumph for Indonesian persistence or even for Dutch patience and forbearance, but under no circumstances is it even a slightly honest triumph for self-determination.

This does not by any means exhaust the list of cases in which the United Nations was confronted with the inconsistencies—conscious or unconscious—of definitions of the term of self-determination. Let us take as examples the case of the Mali Federation and the case of the Belgian Congo. Some may have forgotten that in 1959 the newly independent French African states of Mali and Senegal agreed that they would form an association which they decided to call the Mali Federation. For this, they received general applause; diplomatic recognition was accorded by most of the powers of the world, and they applied for and received United Nations membership for the Federation. However, for reasons that are not important to this story, although of course of overriding importance in the new Federation, a large rift appeared in the structure and they agreed to disagree, finally to the extent of seceding from each other and slashing the bonds that tied them. Although a certain amount of polite concern was expressed, the United Nations quietly accepted the situation, brought Mali and Senegal into membership separately, and little more was said.

Here was a situation where no plebiscite was held either on the creation of the Federation or on its dissolution. No public self-determination was therefore involved, and the governments concerned took the necessary steps, supposedly without objection from the people if not with their outright mandate. One can suppose that in the absence of some kind of violent objection, the United Nations could assume that the principle of self-determination was satisfied. So far, no one has complained!

Now let us look at the Belgian Congo for a contrasting

situation. Here was a new nation set free, perforce prematurely, by the Belgians, who nevertheless strove, in the inadequate time they had, to bring about some semblance of order. To this end, a series of party and tribal conventions was held, and the chief parties of each state of the Congo voted that *the whole Congo would constitute one independent state and that its inhabitants would possess one and the same nationality.* This was in the winter of 1960. It was the closest that the Congolese could possibly come to self-determination under the confusing situation existing then and since, and was certainly much closer than that attained by most of the peoples mentioned earlier.

Yet when Mr. Tshombe, whose own state government had decried the trend toward "splintering off" by tribal leaders, decided to secede from the Congo as a whole, he raised the cry of self-determination, and was supported strongly by certain elements of the Western world. His hopes for recognition from world powers, allowing him to practice his own brand of self-determination, were doomed to disappointment. Not only that, but the United Nations itself rose up in righteousness and decreed that secession in this case was out of the question. And as time went on and both blacks and whites were beaten and even massacred, the United Nations, which had steadfastly held the line of law and order throughout the Lumumba episode and its sequels, found itself in the position first of having to threaten, then to use, force against Tshombe.

Let us bypass for a moment the world and domestic arguments that have raged over the United Nations policy and the United States policy which supported it. These will continue long after these observations will have been forgotten. The main question, you will remember, is the right of self-determination. How does that fit into the Congolese picture? Purely from the point of view of principle, did Katanga have the right to secede? Whose self-determination was involved?

We are reminded that the United States has just celebrated

the centennial of our Civil War, during which Abraham Lincoln directed the fight against the South—not, as many believe, to free the slaves, but to "save the Union." In that ghastly struggle, the principle of "self-determination," as expounded by the South, was overridden by the importance of keeping the United States of America an entity, rather than letting it split into warring segments and perhaps fall prey to what our Soviet colleagues like to call "the colonizers." And in Africa it was obvious to most governments that a Congo hopelessly split by secession of its stronger parts could easily fall prey to outside exploitation—in fact, at least one other Congolese leader seemed to be primed to help the Soviets do the job at the appropriate moment.

And so once more the abstract principle or theory was the victim of political and other considerations, and the right of secession was denied to the Katangese. History may or may not be able to tell us whether our policy and the United Nations policy was right. All we know is that these things were carefully weighed before decisions were reached. In saying this, we are leaving out some collateral considerations that affect the validity of the pure principle in the face of conditions as they exist. The unanimity with which the Katangese themselves felt about a unified versus a split Congo is decidedly in question. The position and reaction of the Balubas and other large tribes, whose primary interests did not include Tshombe's success, would be another.

After this brief trip in search of the meaning of self-determination, we can only conclude that, like many other high-sounding slogans, it is subject to pressure, to modification, to surgery, and sometimes to complete destruction. The people and leaders who seek it may not always realize that it can be fleeting or transitory. Many people, through no fault of their own, have not attained enough political maturity either to have earned it or to use it wisely and successfully. For at its best, self-determination is a tool to be wielded by a sure hand. It will not perform at its best under the impetus of hate, or national ambition, or other more volatile emotions.

Thus it can be seen that a common language like Esperanto is not the answer to communication, even though it might be useful in some ways. The answer lies, somewhat vaguely, in intellectual agreement as to what is right and what is wrong, regardless of the label tied to it. If, after agreement, a label can be affixed, all the better, but you cannot expect the label alone to do the trick. And once the proper label has been affixed, the familiar problem of making deeds live up to words remains.

There is another facet to the double standard of morality that can stand some examination and understanding. Like many of these matters in and about the Glass House, the understanding should not be limited to the United States or the great powers. It should be shared by members of all sizes and ideologies. It is the mistaken way in which most of the Glass House members regard the United States and other powerful members of the free-world group. I am using the United States in these examples because we are in fact the richest and strongest, and therefore the most frequent target for this sort of evaluation.

Put in its simplest terms, a great many—too many—United Nations representatives feel as follows about us: "You [the United States] are the oldest republic among us, the wealthiest nation, one of the two strongest. You say you do not desire territorial or other power expansion; that you want peace and disarmament, decades of progress, the full life, the Great Society, all the rest. If that is all true, you are the leader in such thought and policy, and must be supremely careful always to do the right thing regardless of friends, allies, or your own interests. You have assumed leadership and have therefore taken on responsibilities that demand perfection, not just a good performance. You have maturity and experience and good faith, and you must live up to the image that you have built for yourselves."

Well! This is both flattering and frightening. Flattering because we *do* want people to think well of us—perhaps we want that too much. Frightening because we will have such an impossible time living up to it, and this we do not take in our stride. You hear often of how effective the Soviet propaganda machine is at the Glass House—how they have made it a sounding board of great value compared to what we have been able to do. This is an interesting observation because it has elements of both truth and falsehood in it.

On the "truth" side, yes, the Soviet Union has developed a fairly successful propaganda line. The trouble with it is that it is almost exclusively destructive in nature. It constantly calls names and blackens character. There is no cheer, no hope, no humor—everything is black or white. Anybody who is friendly to the West automatically becomes a "tool of the Wall Street imperialists." But even the negative, critical type of propaganda does have a certain effect, particularly among those who watch the Soviets give speaking and voting support to such causes as anticolonialism, and for whom such support is the alpha and omega of desirability.

But on the "false" side there are many factors, too. A very heavy percentage of the nonaligned nations are fed up with Cold War vilification merely for the sake of calling names. True salesmanship requires a patient and knowledgeable build-up of one's own product rather than a campaign restricted to knocking down the competitor's product. And so the other inmates of the Glass House have two important criteria by which to judge the relative merits of the opposing systems. First, we of the West rarely if ever vilify, and then only when attacked first. We say what we want to say, tell what we want to do, and leave the name-calling to the Communists. Second, the ideology of Communism is so devoid of sensible and constructive ideas of its own that it has sought to beg, steal, or borrow Western concepts and labels, and to distort them for their own purposes. Let no one make the mistake of assuming that newly emergent nations do not know the difference between "democracy" as practiced in the older nations of the West, and the "people's democracy" tag used to cloak the operation of the tyrannical dictatorship of the Communist bloc. They do know the difference as a general rule, and the few that did not realize at first have learned it now, sometimes at heavy cost.

Therefore it is not true that the Soviets have surpassed us in the use of the Glass House as a sounding board; it is my conviction that it is the other way around. This in itself does not free us from the awkward obligations imposed on us by those who claim that because we are mature, experienced, wealthy, and powerful, we should be something more than human. If there is anything that the leaders of a true democratic republic *cannot* do, it is to think and act like supermen.

When your hackles rise, as I do not doubt they must upon occasion, to hear members of the United Nations criticize the United States in bitterest terms for an action that is virtually ignored when the Soviet Union does it, just remember: They expect more of the United States. In spite of mounting and continuing distrust concerning which I speak elsewhere, they still hope and expect that our background and morality will lead us to do the things that *they* think we should, and to refrain from the actions that *they* think wrong. See Vietnam!

There are only three positions that can be taken on issues in the Glass House: in favor, against, or abstention. It is inconceivable that in taking any one of the three stands on any issue of importance, we can make everyone happy. You simply cannot please everybody. One would think, for example, that the United States would receive reasonably handsome applause from all sides for its yearly acceptance of legislative and financial responsibility for the health and welfare of the so-called Palestine refugees. The United States each year doggedly works out a resolution to be adopted on the subject, calling upon United Nations members to support the lives of these unfortunate people. Between them, the United States and the United Kingdom contribute some 90 per cent of all the funds collected by UNRWA for the purpose. The United States contributes 70 per cent, the United Kingdom, 20 per cent.

And do these two "warmongering-colonialist-imperialist-capitalist tools of Wall Street" get any credit for this humanitarian position? Scarcely. The Arab states, who refuse to contribute one cent to the survival of their brothers, attack us because we have not "forced" Israel to accept repatriation of more than a million Arab refugees. The Israelis are unhappy with us because our aid keeps the menace very much alive on their borders, while they think we should "force" the Arab states to absorb the refugees into their own territories. The rest of the non-contributing members wash their hands of responsibility and are glad to let us carry the load.

Far back in the mists of time, some philosophical warrior or athlete or politician was moved to remark that "you can't win them all." Never were truer words spoken. In the Glass House, the United States has come closer to the negation of that adage than anyone could have dreamed. We have had the votes on nearly every fight and we have generally had the right of it—at least enough of the members have thought so. But we cannot expect to win them all, and we should not blame the Glass House if we should occasionally find ourselves in the minority. We struggle under the vast handicap of having people expect more perfection than anyone could deliver—and we must therefore make a special effort to live up to the slogans that have become watchwords for the world, to make them real not only within our country, but within the entire United Nations world. And if we can concentrate on being right rather than popular, and can cling to the ideals that gave us strength, we will win our share.

7 · Myths and Supermyths

WHEN ONE CONSIDERS CHALLENGES to the success or very existence of the United Nations, one must put in the forefront the challenge posed by lack of public support in the member states, or by outright opposition on the part of the public. This disaffection is to be found in nearly every quarter of the globe, and is due to a variety of reasons. One of the most common, of course, arises from disaffection on the part of the government involved. The Security Council or the General Assembly may have taken some action that the government concerned believes to be inimical to its interests. The General Assembly may have insisted upon discussing a matter that a government contends is private and internal; it may have passed a resolution calling upon the government to do something it does not want to do, or to stop doing something that it does want to do. Typical examples of these latter would be the Palestine resolutions; the Kashmir resolutions; the North African resolutions on Tunis, Morocco, and Algeria; the Hungarian resolutions; the Suez resolutions against the United Kingdom, France, and Israel; the Congo resolutions; and the nuclear-testing resolutions aimed at the United States and the Union of Soviet Socialist Republics.

The public opinion of most member states naturally follows the government line to a considerable degree; in some states, it is the only side of a controversy that the public is allowed to learn. It is understandable, therefore, that to the extent that national public opinion sides with its own leadership there can be little consternation, even though we may wish that this were not so.

Occasionally, however, stories get started in member states whose governments strongly support the United Nations—stories that for sheer inventiveness deserve the top prizes for fiction. Being such an open society, with an almost indecent pride in our freedom of speech and of the press, the United States easily outdistances the rest of the members in this doubtful competition. And one of the most interesting factors in the whole business is the extraordinary stamina and vitality of some of the myths that have survived in certain parts of the United States in spite of all the proof to the contrary.

In recent years, I have had the opportunity to do quite a lot of traveling around the country in the course of delivering lectures. I read the local papers on the road, talked to thousands of people, got heckled by a few, and was impressed at the virility and longevity of the following examples of myths: The United Nations is a nest of spies; the United Nations can send our boys to war; the United Nations Military Staff Committee is permanently chaired by a Russian general; our Korean War secrets were given to the Russians at the United Nations; Alger Hiss wrote the United Nations Charter; the Soviets win the Cold War at the United Nations; the United States is the patsy for everybody; the Secretary General is pro-Communist; the Communists effectively keep the United Nations from operating; UNESCO seeks to dominate our educational system and is run by Communists; the United Nations is antichristian; etc., etc., etc.

It will be noted that a large majority of the myths prevalent in the United States are derived from the deep suspicions engendered by the Cold War. There is really very little that can be argued at great length—a story is usually either true or untrue. Those of us who want to believe the worst may well do so in spite of denials, but I can only assure you that I know better, because I was there for eight years. The whole matter of espionage was taken very seriously in the United States Mission to the United Nations; we were in constant touch with the Federal Bureau of Investigation and the State Department's Security Bureau; our phones, our offices, and our residences were regularly inspected electronically and otherwise for any possibility of "bugging" or other types of clandestine surveillance. There is even a story going the rounds that one Delegate's car was successfully "bugged" by another Delegation some years ago, but I could never get proof of it. Obviously neither party in the case would be apt to broadcast the story!

But to return to this whole "nest of spies" complex, I feel that many Americans place far too much emphasis on the comparatively small number of cases that have surfaced, and they have jumped to the conclusion that there must be thousands of cases never discovered. Perhaps we should use a little perspective on this whole business and accept first the fact that it is generally to the interest of member states of the United Nations to know as much as possible about the positions and intentions of all the other members. Certainly the United States is in the forefront of those who need and want to know, because we have such a huge stake involved. It is, therefore, part of every Delegate's job to find out as much as he can without overstepping certain fairly well-recognized lines. These lines preclude theft of documents, wire tapping and bugging, subversion and bribery of other nationals, blackmail, and so on. Occasionally a case is disclosed where such overstepping has taken place, and we can be sure that virtually all of these do eventually come to light.

As this is written, there have been seventeen authenticated cases of *attempted* espionage since 1945 in the United Nations that have come to the attention of the State Department.

Eleven of these cases involved employees of Communist delegations in New York, and six involved employees of the United Nations Secretariat. Considering the number of countries involved and the thousands of employees at and around the United Nations Headquarters, this is indeed a poorly populated "nest of spies." I think it safe to say that in all the great capitals of the world the practice of espionage is more prevalent than here, and in certain recognized listening posts, such as Geneva, Lisbon, and Cairo, the traffic in information is vastly more concentrated and massive than in New York.

As to the United Nations itself, particularly the Secretariat, the pickings for spies are slim, in fact, nearly nonexistent. No one takes important documents to the United Nations. As far as the United States people are concerned, they do not even take State Department position papers to the Headquarters building. Many of these are not highly classified in the first place, and all are liberally quoted in United States speeches on the appropriate subject soon after the opening of debate. Similarly, the average Delegate to the United Nations has little opportunity to talk to Secretariat employees, much less pass them critically classified documents. The overwhelming majority of the employees are dedicated international civil servants. Even if some of them did not wish to heed the rules about carrying on espionage, they would certainly remember that their contracts with the United Nations carry very clear provisions about the performance of their duties. All of them know that apprehension in banned activities would mean automatic permanent dismissal. The few who have tested the system have found this out.

No, by and large the United States does not have to fear the United Nations as a "nest of spies." This does not mean that our guard is ever let down. But the extent of *successful* espionage is so small as to be negligible; United States citizens when approached by a would-be subverter have almost without exception notified the FBI and have worked with that agency to trap the villain; members of Communist Delegations are subject to strict reciprocal control of their movements and travels (in fact, they often complained to me about the surveillance they underwent on a round-the-clock basis). The interests of the American people and their government are in ever-watchful hands.

To deal briefly with some of the other specific charges mentioned above, the United Nations Military Staff Committee is set up by the Charter of the United Nations under the direction of the Security Council. It consists of representatives of the five permanent members of the Security Council, and is, therefore, anti-Communist four to one. But further, this group has never conducted a United Nations military operation and has no immediately foreseeable function in this area; it had nothing whatever to do or say about the Korean operation, the UNEF operation in Palestine, or the ONUC operation in the Congo. It meets once a month for a few minutes and discharges no business. The Chairmanship, thus completely honorary, is rotated every month, and the Committee can ask for only such information as all five members are willing that it should. To characterize this international "appendix" within the United Nations body politic as chaired, dominated, or even influenced by the Soviet Union is clearly absurd.

Yet one occasionally hears a resounding statement to the effect that "It was the Communist military leader of the United Nations who told General MacArthur in Korea that he *must not* cross the Yalu River." I am sure that former President Truman and the Joint Chiefs of Staff at the Pentagon would have been interested to know this, inasmuch as there *is* no Communist military leader of the U.N.

The Korean War was carried on by a special United Nations staff, headed both in New York and in Korea by a United States officer. No Soviet or other Communist personnel participated in any phase of the United Nations Korean operation; the United Nations Military Staff Committee was completely bypassed. The only military information given to the United Nations about the Korean War was decided upon and cleared by the United States Departments of Defense and State before being sent to New York for transmission to the international body. It can thus be seen that any question of passing our military secrets to the Soviets at the United Nations is completely impossible. If the Soviets ever did hear of our intentions before open transmission to the United Nations, nothing they heard could have helped them since all such information became public almost immediately.

Anyone with an elementary knowledge of the United Nations must realize that that body cannot send United States boys to war, cannot commit the United States to any action we believe to be inimical to our interests, and cannot possibly force the United States to do anything we do not want to do. The Security Council of the United Nations can call upon the members to join collective action; the General Assembly can demand, plead, or even decide that certain action is imperative; ECOSOC and the Trusteeship Council can beg, plead, declare, and recommend to their hearts' desire. The fact is that the United States can, if she wishes, turn a deaf ear to all of them. There is nothing in the Charter that can compel the United States to do one single thing she considers to be against her best interests. The idea, somehow still widely held, that the United Nations has power to force obedience is utterly without foundation.

Apparently the purveyors of some of these myths follow a regular pattern. First, they try to find a published statement from someone in the United Nations Secretariat or one of the Specialized Agencies that can be distorted and twisted. After giving the statement this sort of treatment, they elevate it to the status of an official pronouncement of the organization, and then lead good Americans to believe that it is a policy, already decided, which is being carried out all over the world.

The UNESCO myths are good examples. After implying that the principles of UNESCO have been approved by the United States Government (true, in the broadest sense), they then charge the National Education Association, the state and city school boards, the American Association of School Administrators, and the National Congress of Parents and Teachers (PTA) with joining in a plot to brainwash American children for Communism! From there it is, of course, only a short step to the absurd charge that "Moscow Reds" have been in control of American education since the inception of UNESCO.

Not content with this, the myth-makers journey still further into the jungle of vicious calumny. They list names and jobs of high office-holders in the agency. Many of the jobs listed do not exist, certainly not under the titles given; many of the people listed are not even employed in the agency, and some, while listed as "Red lackeys," are well known to the security people of the West as strongly anti-Communist! As a final flick of contempt to our intelligence, we are told that Communists from mainland China, North Korea, North Vietnam, and East Germany help formulate and control the policy of the agency. Of course, the truth is that none of these regimes has ever been a member of UNESCO or indeed of any other agency of the United Nations, and that nationals of these regimes are not even considered for employment in *any* United Nations body. In fact, the Soviets and their sympathizers have often been widely critical of UNESCO for being unfriendly and unresponsive to their interests and demands.

Statistically, you can sometimes find equally mythological statements, such as the one to the effect that "Of the 14 listed UNESCO directors, 11 are from the U.S.S.R., 1 from Hungary, 1 from Yugoslavia, and 1 from France." This sort of thing is perhaps easier to combat, because official statistics exist and can be produced. For one thing, there is no board of directors in UNESCO. There is an Executive Board that serves between policy sessions of the General Conference. It consists of 30 members, of which 3 come from Communist-bloc countries. UNESCO itself has some 1,300 employees, of whom 85 are American, 270 English, and 544 French; only 19 are Soviet citizens.

It has long been a matter of public record that Alger Hiss, in 1945 a member of the staff of the United States Delegation —although not himself a Delegate—could not have colored United States policy in the writing of the United Nations Charter, and did not even attempt to do so. Those who say he did simply do not understand the way these delegations work. There would have been no opportunity for him to make secret deals with Molotov concerning the United Nations Military Staff Committee. Even if he had, such conspiracy certainly ended in ignominious failure, as attested by that body's complete impotence in advancing Communist interests.

As for the Soviets gaining the upper hand in the Cold War through manipulation of the United Nations, the record is simple and clear. As I have said elsewhere, the monotony of their regular and crushing defeats in United Nations voting over the years must be galling in the extreme. On a head-to-head or eyeball-to-eyeball basis with the United States, they have lost literally all of the Cold War conflicts that have been brought before the United Nations for determination. They have found themselves with the majority only in those cases where they have agreed with the West. They have failed to gain their points in such disagreements as disarmament, nuclear testing, the Congo, Hungary, Lebanon, Laos, Korea, West New Guinea, Greece, Iran, and the ICJ opinion on the responsibility for financing peace-keeping operations. All in all, the struggle has been so one-sided that more than one impartial observer has felt it to be unhealthy. Certainly it has not helped endear the United Nations to the Soviet Government or the Russian people.

The other side of this particular coin is the charge that the United States has been and is the patsy for everybody in the whole business. If we define patsy as a slightly moronic, well-meaning cat's-paw who is always held responsible for failure and never for success, it will be difficult to find a case of any importance where this accusation would hold water. I have often felt that the United States viewed its actions in the United Nations too much as a popularity contest instead of as a measure of principles to be admired. However, the charge of allowing ourselves to be led into diverse traps and equivocal situations is simply not tenable.

In the first place, we have been on the winning side of Assembly votes so often that it is monotonous. Even in the few cases where we have been in the minority, the questions have been those of broad recommendations and requests (colonialism, nuclear testing), carrying little stigma and causing only temporary upheavals in our relations with others. The question of whether we have been right in all these matters is not pertinent. We may have been more right in some of our minority votes and abstentions, and wrong in some of our majority actions. Be that as it may, we have never worn the dunce's cap, and where heavy expenditures are involved, we have never found ourselves forced into an equivocal position. Any contributions we make to the United Nations are made at our own initiative, and we do not reluctantly agree to them at the behest of someone else.

Although there are issues where our intentions and our pronouncements are somewhat doubted, we have inevitably been the masters of our own destiny, and we shall continue to be. I personally welcome the "let the chips fall where they may" attitude as long as we know what we are doing. There have been cynical delegates to the General Assembly who have maintained that the only way you can be sure you are right on an issue is when both sides criticize your position! Unfortunately, this rarely happens unless you abstain on a vote and refuse to support any position at all. In that event, you may have been politic or even diplomatic, but no one can

claim that you are "right." A great many members use abstention as a method of demonstrating their distaste for the whole
argument, or their belief that neither side has a monopoly on
virtue. The nonaligned or neutral countries use it in order to
escape the concentrated wrath of one of the disputants. However, though they may escape the concentrated ire of one,
they generally incur the admiration of neither.

As to the accusation of amorality or lack of religion in the
Glass House, this really should not arise at all, unless the critic
involved believes that the entire population of the world
should be converted to one faith only, such as Christianity or
Islam. The Glass House promotes many of the freedoms of
which we Americans are proud in our heritage. Outside of
freedom of speech, which even the best friends of the United
Nations feel is often carried to extremes, the most important
freedom observed is that of worship. All of the world's great
religions are found in the membership of the organization,
and many minor ones as well. No one quizzes another as to
sect or denomination or even over-all religious beliefs, but as
a walk of life, diplomacy seems to carry with it a very deep
conviction of the existence of some sort of supreme being.
Hence we find each Assembly opening and each closing ac-
cented by a minute of silent meditation, to be utilized by each
member in accordance with his own religion. We find a most
impressive Meditation Room near the main public entrance to
the United Nations Headquarters Building, where in completely nonsectarian and silent surroundings each may pray or
meditate according to his own belief. And to underscore the
universal belief in the importance of religion in the Glass
House, by far the favorite of all United Nations anecdotes is
the one in which the late Ambassador Warren Austin of the
United States is supposed to have gently chided the delegates
of Israel and the Arab League in the midst of some of their
more purple passages. Breaking into the flood of invective, he

said: "Come, come, my friends! Let us sit down together and resolve our differences like good Christians!"

No, the Glass House is not a Christian institution, nor was it meant to be, nor should it be. But it is so important to the various religious organizations of the United States that more than thirty religious groups have permanent observers accredited to it, to say nothing of the international groups and groups from other countries. You may hear the accusation that "There is no mention of God in the Charter." This is proper for a political document. Our own Constitution makes no mention of God either.

One of the most persistent of all myths pertaining to the United Nations goes something like this: "The United Nations is just a big international debating society—it never really does anything to keep the peace!" Here the critic is talking about political action, and there is no point in answering him with facts about the work of the Specialized Agencies. This is dealt with in Chapters 2 and 3. But let's look at the record:

In 1946, Soviet troops remained on Iranian territory contrary to treaty provisions. In response to world opinion as expressed through the United Nations Security Council, the troops were withdrawn.

In 1946, Greece complained of Communist assistance to guerrillas infiltrating from Albania and Yugoslavia. A United Nations Peace Observation Commission, sent to the border area, was credited with stabilizing the situation.

In 1947, after violent clashes over the future of the former Italian colonies in Africa, the General Assembly arranged that Libya should become independent, Eritrea federated with Ethiopia, and Somaliland (now independent) was put under United Nations trusteeship.

In 1948, fighting between India and Pakistan over Kashmir was stopped by a cease-fire arranged by the United Nations Security Council. Truce lines were established. A long period of peace ensued, during which negotiations were reopened. Before the bitter fighting of 1965 erupted, a plebiscite had repeatedly been urged.

In 1949, fighting between Indonesia and the Netherlands was stopped by a cease-fire arranged by the United Nations. The new state of Indonesia emerged. In 1962, the United Nations helped negotiations solving the problem of West Irian (New Guinea). Final agreements were arrived at in 1963, and Indonesia took this territory over without warfare.

From 1950 to 1953, United Nations forces in Korea, under the command of the United States, threw back North Korean and Red Chinese invaders, finally stabilized the boundary line, and established the principle of nonforcible repatriation. This was the first demonstration of collective action by United Nations members.

In 1956, General Assembly action halted the British-French-Israeli invasion of Egypt. The small UNEF put into the Gaza Strip is still there, but the situation is relatively quiet.

In 1958, the General Assembly created a special observer group for Lebanon to take over from United States troops that had responded to the Lebanese request for help. All is comparatively quiet.

In 1959, a special United Nations observer team was sent to Laos, easing tensions, and allowing for continuing negotiations. A shaky situation obtained, but official neutral status for Laos has continued.

From 1960 to the present, the United Nations sponsored collective action in the Belgian Congo, which kept the new nation from collapsing and kept the Congo from becoming the Cold War theater. The United Nations is still working under unusual difficulties there.

The 1965 revolt in the Dominican Republic was brought to a nonshooting status by OAS hemisphere troops and a U.N. diplomatic mission which worked with the OAS diplomats in a long and difficult, but finally successful, negotiation.

There is not much to brag about in disarmament programs —but they keep people talking instead of shooting.

The Trust Territories program has been an outstanding success—all but four territories are now independent.

In addition to the successful formation of the IAEA (see Chapter 2), the outer-space committee of the U.N. has done important work.

As to the dated items, focused usually on specific territories, there is of course no way to tell what might have happened if the United Nations had not intervened. In at least eight of these incidents, *shooting was already going on.* In the rest, it was seriously threatened. It would be impossible to make a case that none of these situations held a political danger to the whole world, for we have seen from what comparatively small puffs of smoke a gigantic conflagration can grow.

We should also take cognizance of the fact that United Nations action was not final in some of them; the fighting men are still stationed in the areas they have stabilized, to quickly dampen any sparks that might rekindle. Finally, we should also recognize that in some of these situations the United Nations action, although helpful, was not conclusive. It has been subject to strong criticism, for example, in Palestine, in Korea, in the Congo, and in Santo Domingo.

Yet how are we to evaluate its results at this stage of the world's evolution? What would have happened had we not gone into Korea? And, on the other hand, what might have happened if we had pressed north of the Yalu instead of settling for the Fifty-ninth Parallel? These and many other questions will plague our political-science teachers and our historians for many years to come, and speculation on them can only be idle.

One thing we need not speculate about: In these eleven politico-military incidents that held explosive potentialities for those parts of the world, at least, the United Nations acted. There was no lack of collective courage to face facts. There was plenty of opportunity for pussyfooting to avoid hurting the feelings of friends and allies as well as the noncommitted. But the organization acted, whether everyone approved of the action or not.

Many far less important accusations have been made over the years. Most of them related in some form or other to the major ones listed above. Just in case you should run into some of them from time to time, perhaps I should bring these little myths out into the open. For instance, one can hear or read that "half of the 1,350 administrative executives of the United Nations are Communists or persons willing to follow Communist orders."

Here are the facts: Out of a total of 1,358 executive positions filled as of August, 1964, only 164 were held by the U.S.S.R. and its satellites. According to the agreed quota system, this is only two-thirds of the number to which they are entitled. As to the willingness to take Communist orders, this is not very complimentary to the Australians, Latin Americans, New Zealanders, Japanese, Filipinos, Thai, and other good friends of the West, because nearly one-half of the positions are held by United States, Canadian, and Western European personnel.

Those who disagree with the ONUC have been heard to say: "Khrushchev's approval of the United Nations action in the Congo is proved by the fact that the Soviet Union did not veto it." I wonder where all those who make this criticism were during the fall of 1960. I was at the United Nations. Not only did the U.S.S.R. veto resolutions on the Congo in the Security Council; they forced us to take the issue into a special session of the General Assembly under the Uniting for Peace Resolution. During that session, the U.S.S.R. delegation fought furiously against the Congo resolution and introduced one of its own in opposition. It was not until they realized the overwhelming desire of all the other states to send the United Nations to Leopoldville that they finally withdrew their resolution and abstained, with all their satellites (including Cuba), on the final vote, which came out 70 to 0. This delighted them so thoroughly that they have refused to pay one ruble toward the cost of the operation ever since!

Therefore, in spite of the Hungarys, the Tibets, the Goas, and the other incidents where the Glass House either failed to act successfully or failed to act at all, this record of achievement cannot be gainsaid. And to the extent that it has been an achievement, the myth of the "great debating society that never does anything" is revealed with clarity. In baseball parlance, the Glass House has piled up a lot more hits than strike-outs! The fans ought to be happy.

8 · The United States Wing
of the Glass House

Most Americans get to know the name of the United States Representative to the United Nations, at least the current one if not his predecessors. There are so many occasions when publicity strikes him willy-nilly, and there are other times when he seeks it deliberately for one reason or another. I have discussed elsewhere in broad terms the function of his job. As the Representative of the United States to the United Nations, he has broad responsibility for everything that title implies. He supervises an organization of some 130 employees permanently stationed in New York, and is loaned many dozens more for specific work such as the meetings of the General Assembly, ECOSOC, the Trusteeship Council, and the Security Council.

Under the present system, the Ambassador in charge has two top assistants of ambassadorial rank, one acting as all-around Deputy and second in command, and the other concentrating more or less on Security Council work. There are three other major jobs: the United States Representative to the Economic and Social Council, with the personal rank of ambassador, the United States Representative to the Trusteeship Council, with the personal rank of ambassador, and the Counselor of Mission, who acts as chief of staff for all the other functions of the USUN, as it is usually called. From time to time, other high-ranking personnel appear in New

York to do special assignments. For example, the United States Representative to the Organization of American States may be sent up as special adviser in a Security Council case involving a Latin American nation, or the Chief of the Agency for International Development may arrive to help with a knotty problem before the ECOSOC.

The Economic and Social Council consists of twenty-seven members, including the five permanent members of the Security Council. The United States Representative to this major organ of the United Nations has a minimum staff in New York and derives most of his assistance from Washington. The bulk of these are State Department people, who attend the meetings of ECOSOC in New York each spring and in Geneva each summer. There will be an occasional staff assistant from various other Washington departments: Commerce, Labor, Health, Education, and Welfare, and so forth. The work entails presenting the United States position on all matters of economic and social import that come before the Council; consultation with Council members on the work, reports, and proposals of the various Specialized Agencies; advice to the Chief of Mission and General Assembly delegation on matters before the Second (Economic) and Third (Social) Committees of the General Assembly, and generally riding herd on everything that goes on in this area.

The United States Representative to the Trusteeship Council, like his counterpart in ECOSOC, has only a minimum staff in New York and draws his help almost entirely from Washington. In addition to the inevitable State Department staff members, he may draw heavily upon the Department of the Interior, which is the department charged with the administration of the Trust Territories that are the responsibility of the United States. Unlike his confrère in ECOSOC, he can occasionally rotate into the Chairmanship of the Council, which alternates the chair between administering and non-administering countries from year to year.

Although the work done in ECOSOC and the Trusteeship Council is of vital importance to the United States as well as to the United Nations, the main focus of interest remains on the political stage, where so many fascinating and sometimes frightening dramas are played each year, both in the Political Committee and the Assembly itself. In terms of numbers of troops, the Political Affairs Section of the USUN is notably small, there being only eleven officers in the group. Of course, the top-level people of ambassadorial rank do a great deal of the work with their opposite numbers in the various delegations. It is an understandable rule of thumb that a mid-to-low-ranking officer does not indulge independently in consultation with the ambassador of another United Nations member. At the same time, there must be continuous liaison at the lower levels, and junior officers are often successful in gaining important information from their opposite numbers in the various missions.

Perhaps a brief clarification of the terminology of "Mission" and "Delegation" may be useful. Sometimes, as in the paragraph above, the two are used interchangeably and no one raises any question. Internally in the USUN, one often speaks of calling on the Mission of Argentina or the Argentine Delegation, and means the same thing, or at least the same people. There is, however, a clear difference both in practice and protocol.

The permanent establishment of a country at the United Nations is the Mission. It is not called an Embassy because it is not accredited to any one country. The Chief of Mission in this context is the "Representative" of his country to the United Nations. Depending on the terms of the participation law that his country enacted to bring itself into membership, he is sometimes called "The Permanent Representative of ———— to the United Nations." For our own people, the correct title is "United States Representative (or Deputy Representative) to the United Nations." None of the top diplomats of the members is ever officially called the "Ambassador to the United Nations," although this title is quite often, though incorrectly, used in the United States, in the press or on the speaker's platform. Nor are these people ever properly called "The Delegate of ———— to the United Nations."

The posts of Representative and Deputy Representative of the United States are set up by the statute called the Participation Act of 1945, and those who hold either of these titles are given the official rank of "Ambassador Extraordinary and Plenipotentiary." They are appointed by the President to serve at his pleasure (no fixed term), and must be confirmed in their appointments by the United States Senate. They take their oath separately on this basis, as opposed to the oath taken by "Delegates" to the General Assembly or other official international conferences. "Delegates," therefore, are what the word implies: people who have been delegated to represent the United States on a temporary or term basis to an international meeting. "Delegation" is the term roughly embracing the delegates and their advisory staffs.

The Permanent Representative of a member state of the United Nations is invariably a delegate to the General Assembly each year. Sometimes he is the Chief of Delegation, although quite often that title is assigned to the Foreign Minister or Secretary of State of the country involved. In the United States, the Representative to the United Nations, if slated to serve also as a delegate to the General Assembly, must be nominated for this post by the President, confirmed by the Senate, and sworn in just as though he were a complete stranger to the United Nations job. On one occasion when I was serving as Deputy United States Representative, the nomination list for the General Assembly got so crowded that I was not named on the delegation that year. In spite of this, Ambassador Lodge, with Secretary of States Dulles' blessing, named me as second in command of the team I did not officially belong to, and I served as Chief of Delegation several times when Mr. Lodge was unavoidably absent! Fortunately, no one thought to challenge my right to serve and vote in this capacity.

There has been some argument over the years as to whether the United States Representative should be a professional diplomat or whether, as a political appointee and member of the Cabinet, he should be a politically experienced government official. Since all the United States Representatives have been in the latter category, and since they have garnered considerable public acclaim, it would be difficult indeed to make a strong argument that "our man in New York" should be a career diplomat.

I think that there are two basic arguments in favor of the political approach: First, the subjects that the United States Representative handles are invariably political in nature, and second, the United Nations system, with its General Assembly, its councils and committees, is not unlike the parliamentary systems in our state capitals and in our Congress. It therefore does not seem illogical to assume that a Senator or a Governor or other government official would feel more or less at home at the United Nations, and they do. It is, of course, essential that such a person be backed up by as professional a diplomatic team as he can find, and this is the standard procedure.

In describing the various functions of people in the USUN, it is therefore important to keep the difference in mind, and I shall try to keep the labels straight. The officers of the Political Affairs Section of the Mission are professional diplomats and are largely liaison operators between the Mission and various carefully delineated groups of Missions of other members. Usually these groups are geographical in nature, and have a built-in homogeneity of policy, making it comparatively easy to ascertain the group position on various issues. Thus we find one officer assigned to the Latin American group; another to the NATO countries plus Australia, Canada, and New Zealand; two others assigned to African states; and another to

Asian states. There is usually a Russian-language expert to cover the Soviet-bloc countries, a special expert on the Arab problem, still another expert on disarmament and kindred subjects, and so forth. These officers keep in constant touch with similarly ranked officers in all the other Missions, reporting anything of interest. They must do a certain amount of modest entertaining for which they can sometimes receive partial reimbursement from the "representation fund." This is the fund that Congressman John Rooney, watchdog over the State Department in the House Appropriations Subcommittee, insists on calling "whiskey money," and very badly needed it is, too, but more for food than for drink!

Political officers with substantive rather than geographical functions will, of course, concentrate on those members from states that are appropriate for contact, and they must be thoroughly up to date on all the latest developments. The disarmament expert, for instance, will confine his liaison duties more or less to the members of the seventeen-nation group of the Geneva Disarmament Conference. He must keep his superiors informed on the Geneva situation as well as make reports on any and all attitudes he may detect among other Missions.

When the General Assembly is not in session, the pace is a good deal slower, but the United States Mission can never really look forward to or enjoy a quiet period, except in a relative sense. There is always some committee or commission or board or agency meeting in New York that demands attention and service of one kind or another. During the average year, the USUN services more than 2,000 such meetings. And if at times the pressure of meetings and consultations with other Missions should abate somewhat, there are always the individuals and groups and delegations from United States organizations that want briefings and lectures and tours of the Glass House.

When the General Assembly meets, the entire life of the

Mission is turned over to the session. The population of employees is swelled, almost alarmingly, by the influx of delegates, advisers, assistants, and experts. Some of the latter move to New York for the full session, while others shuttle back and forth on special assignments. The traffic in phone calls and telegrams and cables quadruples. During the first week or ten days, the crowding and confusion is at its height, because the Secretary of State is expected to attend, for conferences and meetings with bigwigs from overseas, and often to deliver the United States address in the so-called General Debate.

At any rate, this twelve-week period of the General Assembly, sometimes carried over after New Year's, is the time when the Mission is properly known as the "Delegation," since it houses and devotes virtually all of its time to the Delegation of ten members to which each General Assembly member is entitled. They have had a two-day briefing in Washington on the various subjects that are to be taken up at the Assembly, or, as many of them have admitted, "just enough briefing to be thoroughly confused." This means that there must be in constant attendance experts from State and other departments in all the varied subjects represented on the agenda. The two congressional members of the Delegation, alternated year to year between members of the Senate Foreign Relations Committee and the House Foreign Affairs Committee, generally bring in at least one assistant from the appropriate committee staff as well.

For purposes of organizing the Delegation for its exacting work, two major bodies are generally set up. First, there is the Delegation itself, with its expert advisers. A meeting of the "Delegation" is usually held two or three times a week during the General Assembly. The attendance at such meetings will run from sixty to seventy-five people, comprising the top staff of the Mission and the advisers to the Delegation, as well as the Delegates themselves. The meetings are organized to give full play to two major aspects of the work: briefing and information to the Delegates, and reaction opinion from the Delegates. At these occurs the interplay of policy statement, criticism, and applause that normally attends the democratic process as we understand it.

Each delegate is invariably asked for his opinion after a discussion or briefing session. Although it is thoroughly understood that the Delegation is "instructed"—that is to say, takes its orders from Washington and carries them out—there is always the possibility, more often realized than one might think, that the collective opinion of the group may change the position adopted by the policy-makers. I have several times watched, and a few times presided over meetings where strong disagreement has arisen as to the position papers issued as instructions to the Delegation. In such cases the Chief of Delegation may name a subcommittee of the group to draft a message to the State Department setting forth the argument and whatever alternative position may represent their beliefs. Or he may take it upon himself or delegate his Deputy to transmit the disagreement to Washington. In unusually difficult situations, he may even carry the word in person to Washington, but this is rare indeed.

In any event, the Delegation, even though instructed and quite often docile, has the right and the machinery to question the judgment of the Washington policy-makers, all the way to the top. I said earlier that this happens more often than one might think, but perhaps that is too strong an implication. It does happen, but how often "one might think" is a relative term, and my guess would be that once or twice a session would be a reasonably accurate estimate as to how often the United States Delegation disagrees strongly enough with the State Department to put the machinery of dissent into motion. When it does feel that strongly, it has a good chance of success.

The other major body, whose main function is to keep the Delegation moving smoothly and without undue harassment through the rapids and shoals of the session, is sometimes called the Delegation Staff, to indicate the difference between it and the so-called Mission Staff. During some of the General Assemblies of my tenure, the State Department even sent up a fairly high-ranking officer to be the Chief of that Staff, although this is not regularly done now. The idea was, and still is, simple: Here is a meeting of more than one hundred sovereign nations, gathered to discuss perhaps eighty to one hundred items to be assigned to seven permanent committees. A small nucleus of United States people are assigned to each committee, and another small group is assigned on an *ad hoc* basis to each item. It is of major importance that the Chief of Delegation not lose track of what a committee might be doing on a certain subject, and of no less importance to have him and the appropriate officials of the State Department keep track of how the responsible appointees are doing with their prescribed duties in connection with each job.

The Delegation Staff, therefore, has to meet with considerable frequency to catch up with all these details, to evaluate progress or results or both, and to formulate plans and procedures for dealing with whatever situations may arise. These men and women are thoroughgoing professionals, including most of the senior staff at the United States Mission to the United Nations and all the senior staff members assigned from Washington or other parts of the world to the General Assembly.

Up to this point, we have described the ECOSOC group, the Trusteeship group, and the Political Affairs group of the New York headquarters of the USUN, plus the additional experts and delegates who swell the ranks every year for the General Assembly. There are many other people in the USUN with vitally important jobs who never make the headlines. Without them, you have a fine-looking bunch of chiefs, but you do not have the hard-working subchiefs and Indians who keep the machinery operating. In an army, we are told, each soldier on the firing line has a dozen or more military and civilian men and women working full time to keep him going. To a certain extent, this is true of the diplomat on the United Nations firing line, and the rest of this chapter will concentrate on the support forces that make the USUN political and other task forces operative.

The Public Affairs Division consists of a Director of Public Affairs, a Director of News Services, and a Director of Public Services, two Public Affairs Officers, an Information Specialist, together with appropriate secretarial assistance. Their job is, of course, to present the best possible image of the United States to the United Nations, to all other countries, and to the United States public. It is hard to say which of the three areas is the most important, but I lean toward the last one. Everyone will admit, I suppose, that the United Nations would not survive for long if American public opinion became seriously opposed to it. American public opinion needs constant attention and care, due to our vaunted freedom of speech and other freedoms, which allow people to say the most outrageously untrue things about the United Nations and our positions in regard to many of the issues we face there. This phenomenon is discussed in Chapter 7.

Next in importance, I believe, comes the question of presenting the right image to the rest of the world, particularly inasmuch as the propaganda mills of the Soviet bloc work overtime in the United Nations as well as around the world. The USUN's job, therefore, involves maintaining the best possible relations with foreign newspaper correspondents for stories to be filed out of New York, and also sending materials to Washington to be distributed through USIA, the Voice of America, and our press officers in United States embassies throughout the world. Make no mistake about it: The war of the printed and spoken word is a tough one. Our opponents are, in the main, utterly unscrupulous about distortion of fact; the more fanciful their flights of imagination concerning our policies and actions, the more credit they get at home. Never can we afford to let down our guard.

The job of representing our position strictly to the United Nations is at least more simple, though difficult enough. At the U.N. are the accredited correspondents of all of the major wire services covering the various members of the organization; here, too, are the representatives of the OPI (Office of Public Information) of the United Nations itself. Here are the special correspondents of newspapers from all corners of the world. They are available for open press conferences; they are available for mimeographed or special releases; they are available for phone calls and for an occasional lunch or a convivial drink. There is virtually no rule of thumb more important to a United States Representative than that of becoming and remaining easily accessible to the United Nations press corps; the first sign of inaccessibility is enough to start the "grumbles" going. Once they start, it takes untold work to recover lost ground—in fact, the ground lost is rarely fully regained.

Hence the work of the officers in the Public Affairs Division is of the utmost importance, just as the work of a Hagerty, Salinger, or Moyers is so important to an Eisenhower, Kennedy, or Johnson. The United States Representative must be nimble and newsworthy; he and his top assistants must be articulate yet discreet. The whole Mission and Delegation must be carefully briefed on what to say, how to say it, and to whom. In these days, when communication to the farthest-flung parts of the world is virtually instantaneous, it takes the utmost in skill and application merely to keep from making unfortunate mistakes, to say nothing of putting your best foot forward.

The Director of Public Affairs is naturally the Chief of the Division, and it is self-obvious that the Director of News Services must be in charge of purely press and other media relations. The Director of Public Services, however, is another of those unsung heroes who generally works under a blanket of anonymity as far as the papers and wire services is concerned. He is the person who must work directly with the American public, both on an individual and collectively organized basis. While I was in New York, this position had responsibility for what was called "public mail," phone calls to the Mission (rather than to an individual), calls or visits by individuals and groups in search of information, experience, or the satisfaction of curiosity, or being able to say that they went personally to the Mission and talked to an officer there.

"Public mail" from the general populace to the Mission or the Chief of Mission on broad issues can become relatively heavy. Form letters, form telegrams, petitions, and the like are assigned here for acknowledgment or reply, depending on the policy question involved. Scores to hundreds of these are handled per day, and are generally signed by the Director or one of his officers, since it would be impossible for the Chief of Mission to find the time to sign them himself, and no employee should be allowed to sign the Chief's name to correspondence. Individual "crank" letters, often sent by sincere people who are convinced that they hold the answer to world peace and so on, must also be handled most tactfully by the Director. We always made it a rule that each of these, no matter how "far out" it seemed to be, should be read with great care. One never knows when a modern version of "out of the mouths of babes and sucklings" might provide the germ of a really useful idea.

Another most important part of the work of the Public Services Director is the communication line that he keeps open to organizations interested (generally favorably) in the United Nations and in United States participation and policy. These run all the way from correspondence with the second grade of an upstate New York school to arranging for the annual visit of the Canadian War College. He must keep in close touch with the nongovernmental organizations (the

NGO's). These organizations, consisting of labor, civic, veterans, women's, religious, racial, and many other groups, are accredited to the United Nations and are issued passes for official observers and other officers in order to facilitate their entering certain parts of the headquarters normally closed to the public. Among them, they represent upward of 60,000,000 United States citizens and, as such, can and do exercise considerable influence on public opinion. During my day, we also organized visits to New York by groups of business leaders each week, usually on a localized geographical basis. This proved most valuable as a public-opinion factor because of the prominence of the members of the group in each community that set the trip up, and I hope that the present incumbents at the USUN are carrying this on in one form or another.

Press, photo, radio, and television coverage weave their way through all of these activities, and there is also the serious business of helping a researcher, or a student preparing a thesis, or a writer looking for a specific angle on some phase of the international organization. Speech-writing and researching are, of course, a continuing and standard operating procedure. This takes shape in every conceivable way: from original research and drafting to the final polishing of a penultimate text sent up from Washington in response to dozens of rewrite suggestions made in New York and elsewhere. Speeches, statements, and releases are not by any means the sole product of the Division, but they rank very high in importance, because they form the basis on which United States policy is broadcast to the world.

One of the most important independent Divisions of the United States Mission to the United Nations is the group known today as "International Organization Affairs." I shall describe later the existence and importance of the "Headquarters Agreement" between the United States and the United Nations, carrying as it does the entire load of the problems that beset both the United States and the Secretary

General of the United Nations. The Division of International Organization Affairs has a fantastically difficult job in the representation of the "host country" to the United Nations itself and each of the missions and delegations of the member states. The difficulty will not readily be understood by those not thoroughly familiar with diplomatic procedure, but should be tagged as the processes and procedures whereby the United Nations and all its members are persuaded to live up to and observe the laws of the cities, counties, and State of New York as well as those of the United States.

This Division provides service to all the 116 non-American missions and delegations in scores of different ways. Its Director is a lawyer thoroughly versed in all the ramifications of the Headquarters Agreement. He is the main legal liaison between the United Nations Secretariat and the United States Mission. He is also the main legal liaison between all other missions and the governments of the City of New York, and the Federal Government insofar as domestic law is concerned. Problems? You name them; they have them. First in volume are the various traffic violations, of which illegal parking is by far the most common. It seems hard for some of our guests from overseas to realize that there are some places where even a "DPL" license plate is not allowed to park, in front of fire hydrants, for instance, or double-park in a narrow street for three to four hours.

It is common knowledge, of course, that certain courtesies are shown United States diplomats overseas, and that reciprocal courtesies must therefore be shown our distinguished visitors to the United Nations. It may annoy our local police forces to some extent, and also some of our local tax collectors, but there it is. Reasonable leniency is exercised by the cop on the beat depending on the violation, but it is rare that a violation that is considered really serious when committed by an American can be shrugged off when committed by a foreign diplomat. It is therefore not unusual for tickets to be issued to diplomats in these cases. Some of them are accepted with equanimity (part of the expense budget of many Missions includes an item for the payment of local fines and collateral as an inescapable part of the expenses of the Mission). Given the traffic and parking congestion on the narrow streets of New York, the official visits of Mission personnel to other Missions scattered about the city are seriously hampered, and some of the personnel are almost forced into temporary illegal parking in order to get their jobs done.

On the other hand, certain Missions are notoriously lax in their observance of perfectly reasonable traffic laws and regulations. Some of them will collect several tickets without answering a single summons. More than once during my duty in New York I was forced to remind Mission Chiefs of various countries that they were expected to live up to the rules of New York, just as our people were expected to live up to the rules in their capital cities. All these matters, plus others both serious and hilarious, keep this Division on its toes and hustling. There are tax matters, and disturbances of the peace running from quiet picketing through chicken-plucking in hotel rooms to attempted murder. There are crude attempts at blackmail, not-so-crude attempts at espionage, cases of sex both normal and deviate, drunken driving, assault by yoking and mugging, and many others.

Not all of the work of the Division of International Organization Affairs is concerned with wrongdoing. There are many other services that the Mission regularly provides. There are arrangements for the assignment and distribution of diplomatic license plates for upward of 800 cars belonging to non-Americans. There are arrangements for special travel in the United States. There are services to help newly arrived diplomats find both office and living space in or near New York.

In cooperation with the Bureau of International Organization Affairs in the State Department, there is a large area of responsibility in continuous liaison with the Secretariat of the

United Nations. Most of these have to do with the proper implementation of the Headquarters Agreement. All arguments about granting entry into the United States are funneled through this organization, as well as those having to do with the exit, forced or otherwise, of undesirables. The United Nations receives many complaints from visiting delegates about the treatment received in New York or on Route 40 or in almost every conceivable place and situation within our boundaries. There are also boundary limits placed on representatives of Communist nations, by which we of the United States reciprocate against travel restrictions placed on our diplomatic personnel in those particular countries.

There is also a large area of work connected with the administrative side of the United Nations. The Chief of the Division of International Organization Affairs, for instance, represents the United States on the twelve-man United Nations Advisory Committee on Administrative and Budgetary questions—a busy little part of the plant, and one whose work is far more important than it is advertised to be.

Virtually all the rest of the employees and functions of the United States Mission to the United Nations reside in the Division of Administrative Affairs, which consists of what might be called the "Office Manager" headquarters and four sections performing duties in reference and research, reporting, communications, and general services. There are sixty-six individuals in all, thus comprising by far the largest group at the Mission, and bearing out again the truism that it takes many heads and hands to keep the combat soldier on the firing line.

The Chief Administrative Officer is the Office Manager of the Mission, and as such has myriad details of varied importance to oversee. He supervises the Protocol Officer, whose job is to arrange for all the different kinds of entertainment events undertaken by the top Mission officers and, during the General Assembly, the members and top staff of the Delegation. Issuance of invitations, responses to invitations, menus, and seating arrangements are perhaps small details, but they are of the utmost importance in the diplomatic world. To neglect acknowledgment of an invitation is as serious as to omit inviting certain proud (I suspect that "touchy" might be a better American adjective) individuals. Serving the wrong kind of food or drink at the wrong times or dates to the wrong people can get you into as much trouble as an unfavorable vote in the Security Council. And as for seating! Diplomats are so sensitive on the protocol of seating that some have been known to walk out of a dinner party in high dudgeon when they felt insulted by their placement at the table. In addition to the protocol of seating by seniority and rank, seatings have to be planned with extreme care in order to avoid unfortunate juxtapositions in the political, religious, and racial fields. With all the hard feelings rampant around the world, it is no wonder that a protocol officer once told me that he was regularly afflicted with a "wake-up screaming" nightmare, in which he was forced to arrange a table-seating to accommodate the representatives of India, Pakistan, Nationalist China, Syria, Israel, Cuba, Ghana, and the Republic of South Africa!

The Office Manager staff also includes the Personnel Officer of the Mission, whose duties are those of the usual personnel officer in the hiring and placement of employees. The United States Mission to the United Nations adheres to the personnel practices of the State Department, although there are certain exceptions from the former's hard-and-fast rules. The Civil Service regulations are generally applied, but the exigencies and peculiarities of the post make it necessary to waive them at times for specific employees who are needed for specialized reasons. But keeping records on a group of one hundred thirty employees ranging from laborer to Class I Ambassador is not the easiest job in the world, and the person in this spot may well yearn occasionally for a more humdrum post elsewhere in the government.

The financial side of the Mission's administration is generally entrusted to the Administrative Officer, who serves as deputy to the Chief Administrative Officer. All questions of annual budget, salaries, wages, annual leave, sick leave, disbursement of entertainment funds, purchase and repair of machinery, equipment, and supplies come under his watchful eye. He has a budget and fiscal assistant and a budget and fiscal clerk to help him, and he has responsibility for the proper disposition of the funds resulting from an annual appropriation of approximately $1,300,000.

There are several other functions in the Administrative Offices section that should receive brief mention. There is, for instance, the first-aid and hospital room, which is presided over by a registered nurse and boasts a thoroughly equipped dispensary with beds and basic medical necessities short of doctors' care. There is the travel clerk, who is responsible for all the reservations for travel and hotels to be used by representatives of the USUN; the watch officer, who takes care of all calls of whatever nature that come in after regular office hours. Most of the calls are for the top officers of the Mission and all of them insist on having someone in the Mission know where they can be reached in an emergency. In addition to these are individuals with self-descriptive titles such as receptionist, correspondence clerk, secretarial assistant, and so forth.

Also in this division, there is a Reference and Research Section of some eight specialists whose job it is to gather and file all kinds of information that could prove useful to the top officers of the Mission. What was the vote on the resolution of 1948 having to do with the Baruch Atomic Energy Plan? What did Ambassador Warren Austin say in his speech about the Palestine question in 1950? Who sponsored the Disarmament Resolution that passed unanimously in 1954? On what subjects did the Soviet Representative cast a veto in the Security Council from 1950 through 1956? In what year was Japan admitted to the United Nations? Outer Mongolia?

North Vietnam?* The Reference and Research Section can produce the answers. They are invaluable in helping to draft speeches and statements, in compiling briefs for the Chief of Mission's consultations, in answering congressional queries— in fact, in anything requiring that someone get the facts.

Another section that blooms unnoticed in the desert air is the Reporting Section. Its major job is to compile and send the State Department a daily report on everything that happens at the United Nations in which the United States has an interest. Considering the fact that the United States has some interest in just about everything that happens on any given day, this job is no sinecure. In addition to the daily reports to the State Department, this Section also notifies the Reference and Research Section about important statements, votes, amendments, resolutions, and parliamentary maneuvers that have taken place or have been offered or discussed or debated or passed. The United States Mission to the Glass House can ill afford to be badly informed, and these two sections see to it that it cannot happen here.

Next comes the Communications Section, composed of some twenty-four machine operators, supervisors, clerks, and messengers. The bulk of their work is in sending properly encrypted telegrams to Washington and in receiving and delivering properly decrypted or decoded messages to Mission officers. This is a fascinating section, with the major part of its work done behind locked and bolted steel doors. Not a cloak-and-dagger outfit itself, it must nevertheless translate all classified messages *into* the secret code of the State Department before sending them out, as well as *from* the secret code as they come in. These codes are not subject to "breaking" by espionage agents of foreign powers, since the messages are transmitted and received by direct wire with Washington. It is when coded messages are sent by radio telegraph or tele-

---

* Yes, I know that North Vietnam has never been a member. So does the Research Section!

phone that they are in danger of interception and possible "breaking." The USUN does not use wireless transmission, and although an overseas phone call might be occasionally monitored by others, one always takes care not to say anything that should not be overheard.

The breaking of codes is, of course, one of the most common methods of successful espionage, and the possibility is quite taken for granted even among representatives of friendly powers. Many smaller countries and indeed the United Nations itself have often used the so-called International Code, with variations, because of the expense and difficulty of developing a world-wide network of operators skilled in the use of special codes. I remember one day talking with Secretary General Hammarskjöld, who had many years of diplomatic experience behind him before coming to New York. He was jokingly referring to the probability that several member nations had been able to read messages he had sent to his representative in the Congo, and genially included the United States among those privy to the code. Pretending astonishment, I asked if he expected me to admit it, and asked him in turn whether his cryptographers had been able to read our messages. He replied with a twinkle that of course he could no more answer such a question than I could, but added that he would be very much surprised if it were not the case on our side, since the good old International Code was, after all, fairly well known.

The last Section in the Administrative Division is somewhat of a catchall called the General Services Section. Here resides the duplicating unit, which mimeographs and otherwise reproduces all necessary documents; the telephone unit, which boasts what I consider easily the best group of switchboard operators I have ever known; the labor group, which sees to the installation, moving, and removal of all furniture and fixtures, including phones, intercoms, office equipment, carpeting, and the like; and the long-suffering chauffeur group, whose job it is to transport V.I.P.'s and documents all over New York, usually through the thickest traffic. The question of official transportation for the top officers of the Mission has undergone a great deal of scrutiny and criticism, particularly on the part of congressional committees. There used to be terrific squabbles over the "official car" items in the budget of the USUN. Since the Participation Act called for two full Ambassadors, it would be expected that each would be provided with prestigious transportation. Such was not the case, alas, and the prestige of the United States was truly suffering when I first took up my duties in February of 1953.

It seems that budget requests for the preceding several years had hopefully included items for new cars for the top brass, only to have them struck out by the State Department, the Bureau of the Budget, or the Congress. I found, therefore, that Ambassador Lodge was riding around in a singularly tired and somewhat shabby 1949 Cadillac, whereas I, as the Deputy, rejoiced in a vastly underpowered Chrysler Windsor, vintage of 1947. Secretary Dulles was less than impressed with these chariots upon his first visits to New York, and used to prefer riding in a rented limousine of more recent origin. Thus it came to pass that the following budget year found the Secretary of State, the Under Secretary of State, and United States Representative to the United Nations, and the Deputy United States Representative to the United Nations the proud passengers in four brand-new gleaming Cadillac limousines. The answer? Not to be found in a beneficent bureaucracy or a kinder Congress. These cars did not even belong to the United States Government, but were leased from General Motors for a sum so reasonable that not even the hardest-hearted official could fail to agree that it was good for the country even though it might not have been good for General Motors! And so, I imagine, it is to this day, on the basis of a new car each year.

9 · Working Week at the Glass House

THE WORK THAT GOES ON from day to day at the United States Mission to the United Nations, particularly during the sessions of the General Assembly, far exceeds the scope of what was envisioned in the U.N. Charter or in any organizational manual. The following, therefore, is the story of a typical working week as I knew it, both as deputy to Ambassador Lodge and during the period when I was Chief of Mission. It is possible that the Mission operated differently under Ambassadors Austin and Gross, our predecessors, and under my successors, Ambassadors Stevenson and Goldberg. I say this because I have no intention of describing somebody else's job, particularly since I have had no opportunity to observe how other people run the show. To begin with, a bit of background.

The first thing to remember is that the Mission is unique; it has no counterpart anywhere in the United States Foreign Service. The one that comes nearest is the office of the United States Representative to NATO in Paris, but that does not come very close. In New York, across the street from the Glass House, stands the only United States Embassy in the United States. The Great Seal of the United States is over the door of the building, as it is over the door of the Embassy residence on the forty-second floor of the Waldorf Towers at Fiftieth Street and Park Avenue. The Ambassador not only represents the United States at the United Nations; he is also the representative of the host country to all the delegations and to the United Nations Secretariat. There is a regular treaty signed by the United States Government and the United Nations that governs the relationship between the host country and the organization. It is called the Headquarters Agreement, and spells out the obligations of each party to the other.

To this extent, it is, rather than merely a Mission, a quasi-formal extension of the United States State Department in matters having to do with the United Nations. Many people do not realize that the hundreds of delegates who come from other countries are diplomatically accredited, in the strict sense of the term, not to the United States but to the United Nations. The United States cannot refuse entry into this counry of any properly accredited person under the Headquarters Agreement unless it can be shown that he is coming for purposes outside that agreement or seriously inimical to the host country. A person can be expelled only for the same reasons, and the expulsion is nearly always channeled through the Secretary General, who notifies the chief of the delegation concerned that a certain individual is *persona non grata*.

There are also careful arrangements made through the United States Mission on relations with the government of the City of New York and the State of New York—matters of taxation, municipal services, and state supervision—discussed in the preceding chapters.

One other fact makes this job unique: It automatically carries with it rank as a member of the Cabinet of the President of the United States. President Eisenhower started this precedent with Ambassador Lodge, and continued it with me. Presidents Kennedy and Johnson have continued it with Ambassadors Stevenson and Goldberg, and it is my prediction and hope that this status will continue to accrue to the job. It is of vital importance, in "selling" the American position, that the rest of the United Nations members realize that the United States Representative is privy to the inner councils of his government.

One other matter that might be useful as background: The agenda of the General Assembly session is usually made up of more than seventy separate items, each of which will be considered by the appropriate committee. The head of the United States Delegation rarely handles more than a half-dozen of these, but those he personally handles are usually Political Committee items of major importance. The other nine members of the Delegation are assigned at the outset to specific items in specific committees, although they practice flexibility to whatever degree is necessary. I mention this point to explain why this story of a week's work seems to cover comparatively few of the burning issues before the United Nations.

The first two weeks (at least) of every Assembly session are taken up with what is called the General Debate. I had a hard time getting used to this term because although it is certainly "general" enough, it is far from being a "debate" as we understand the term. It is a series of speeches by the heads of Delegations, setting forth the ideas of their respective countries on every conceivable subject in the international field. Since most of the speeches last half an hour to an hour and there are now 117 speeches, you can see that very little else can be done during that period.

One of the wildest General Debates in memory was that in the fall of 1960—the famed Khrushchev shoe-pounding days. It was the lot of Ireland's much-liked and much-respected Frederick H. Boland to be President of the Assembly during that stormy session.

Among the various incidents he surmounted with skill and calm, one stands out above all others in my mind. The debate had been gaining in temperature by the minute, with points of order and shouted recriminations alternating in furious sequence. The climax came when the representative from an East European member nation was at the rostrum. Several delegates, overheated by his scathing references to their governments, called points of order on him. He refused to obey the rules and allow the objectors' points to be made, even though President Boland several times requested him to do so. The tension and the noise rose and rose until Boland, taking an extra-firm grip on his gavel, brought it down with such force that the head split and flew off the handle, barely missing the speaker's head.

Almost instantly the uproar stilled, as if everyone was holding his breath. Then a roar of laughter broke out at the sight of President Boland, with empurpled face, holding the short stub of gavel handle uselessly above the pounding block. He joined in the laughter and sent out for a spare gavel. But he scarcely had to use the new gavel at all, so docile had the Assembly become. Later, the United Nations Correspondents' Association, at a dinner in Boland's honor, gave him a large basket of tiny gavels, each with a kelly-green ribbon. He thereupon presented one to each of the delegates who had been embroiled in the affair, and the little green decorated gavel still occupies a place of honor in my collection of memorabilia.

Fortunately, no one expects to accomplish anything during the General Debate, so the turbulent opening of the 1960 session did not set progress back too far. The real work of the Assembly starts after the General Debate has concluded. I have, therefore, picked for my hypothetical "week" a Monday-through-Sunday period late in October, sometime between 1955 and 1960, when the Assembly is getting its teeth into important matters and the protocol officers of the various delegations have organized their social schedules. So, with a deep breath, here goes! My diary for the period would read thus:

Monday, 9:00 A.M. Top Mission staff meeting, forecasting action for the week, planning assignments and separation of duties, particularly visiting staff from Washington. Received weekend reports of traffic and other difficulties of various delegations, instructed legal counsel to set up meeting with Police and Traffic Commissioners later in week.

9:30 A.M. Full Delegation meeting—gave briefing on the disarmament item starting this morning in Political Committee. General discussion of United States position paper on this subject; many questions. Delegation and advisers agreed that little could come of debate; that United States should "hold the line" and keep in close touch with British, French, Canadians, Italians, and Russians.

10:00 A.M. Brief consultation with British and French in regard to disarmament; agreed United States would speak first, other Western members to follow after Soviet line had become apparent. United Kingdom agreed to talk to Canadians and Italians in accordance with above; it is understood that Soviet may not speak until tomorrow.

10:30 A.M. Committee 1 (Political) opens debate on disarmament; first speaker on the list—Brazil. I then made major presentation in behalf of the United States and Western members of disarmament negotiating group, a speech lasting about forty-five minutes. Several delegations that had inscribed to speak announced they would like time to study the United States statement. Saudi Arabia spoke briefly.

12:00 NOON. Left Committee 1 to keep appointment with group of Senators and Congressmen who had been visitors to the United States Delegation at the arms talk in Geneva. Long discussion; some disagreement with United States position. Suggested they take up argument with State Department.

12:50 P.M. Back to Committee 1 in time to hear last few minutes of somewhat critical talk by Sweden. The Swedish Representative apparently does not think the major antagonists are trying hard enough to find agreement.

1:00 P.M.   Luncheon by Representative of Peru in honor of his Foreign Minister, who is returning to Lima tomorrow. Many kind and graceful remarks from latter; President of General Assembly responded for the United Nations; I for host country. Soviet Representative, seated next to me, made mild remarks about my disarmament presentation—told me he did not know whether he would speak this afternoon or not. Polish Representative, upon completion of the luncheon, said that he thought Soviet would speak.

2:30 P.M.   Gave brief talk to nongovernmental organization group on subject of disarmament posture. Considerable dissatisfaction with United States position as being too rigid. Told them to wait and hear the Soviet position before passing judgment.

3:00 P.M.   Committee 1 afternoon session, with Soviet speaking second after Argentina. Long, involved, somewhat disorganized presentation, caused largely by desire to rebut my speech while giving his own. Tone not too violent, but full of "never," "impossible," "totally unacceptable," etc. Sent word to him asking for a consultation.

4:30 P.M.   Brief consultation with Soviet Representative. Suggest that in order to clarify for all members, we work up a joint statement showing areas of agreement and areas of disagreement. He agreed that this would be better than asking all members to dig through our long speeches for themselves, thus probably developing inaccurate picture of points at issue. Assigned drafting of statement to appropriate high-level staff.

5:00 P.M.   Back to Committee 1 just in time for the closing gavel—no more speakers ready. Told British, French, Canadians, Italians about agreement on joint statement; arranged to have them see draft before approval but doubted many changes needed since positions reasonably clear after Geneva and Washington talks. Nongovernmental organization representative admitted United States no more rigid than Union of Soviet Socialist Republics. Up to the cubbyhole office at the United Nations to handle mail, hear staff and other reports from other committees, luncheons, hall conversations, etc.

6:00 P.M. With Mrs. Wadsworth to Iranian reception at Plaza Hotel. Rather perfunctory comments on speech, since all old stuff. Several Representatives of "nonaligned" countries hinted they would like to see more flexibility on the part of the United States and the Union of Soviet Socialist Republics. Asked them what they were ready to do with their own military forces. No answer.

6:45 P.M. With Mrs. Wadsworth to Venezuelan reception at Ambassador's residence. Same general-type conversation. Latin American countries willing to talk big disarmament but most have enough worries near home and are not anxious for loss of defense capability. One Representative of a neutral country expressed opinion United Nations debate on disarmament no possible use this year. Privately, silently agreed. Escaped in time to dress for dinner.

8:00 P.M. With Mrs. Wadsworth to dinner given by the Foreign Minister of the United Arab Republic at the St. Regis Hotel. Very unusual dinner in that the only guests are United States Delegates and officials and their wives. Much very frank discussion around the table and consensus was that gathering was of great value in clarifying positions and reasons therefor.

11:45 P.M. To bed.

Tuesday, 9:00 A.M. Top Delegation and Mission staff meeting. Checked out all reporting telegrams of previous night, which, as usual, were not completed until midnight. Checked in all incoming telegrams from Washington and other parts of the world giving reaction reports to disarmament and other presentations. Rehashed all possible important tips gathered during previous day's official meetings, receptions, dinners, Delegates' Lounge conversations, etc.

10:00 A.M. Consultation with the Representative of the Netherlands. Subjects: disarmament, West New Guinea.

10:30 A.M.   Meeting with group of hotel and apartment-house managers on subject of finding living and office quarters for Asian and African diplomats and their staffs. Realty men very cooperative in attitude but still gloomy on the reaction of owners and tenants. Agreed that they would continue to stress Federal Government determination to overcome discrimination wherever found.

11:00 A.M.   Committee 1 for resumption of debate on disarmament. Speeches by Denmark, Mexico, Ceylon, and the Philippines. Strong feeling of "a plague on both your houses." Staff reports that draft of joint East-West statement agreed upon yesterday is going well, may be ready for tomorrow.

1:00 P.M.   Luncheon given by Representative of Australia in honor of his Foreign Minister, who is leaving for Canberra tomorrow. Almost entirely social gathering, except that several Commonwealth Representatives warned against some kind of a "ploy" planned by the Soviets. No solid information, but enough rumor to set all the antennae quivering.

2:30 P.M.   Briefing for members of the National War College, in the Trusteeship Chamber. Intensely keen and intelligent group with many searching questions. A really stimulating outfit to discuss things with.

3:00 P.M.   Consultation with the Foreign Minister of Ireland, who has decided to concentrate on stopping the spread of nuclear weapons to countries not now possessing them. Gave me a draft of a resolution on the subject to pass along to Washington.

3:30 P.M.   Rather than get hooked into the debate in the First Committee, arranged emergency meeting of Western disarmament representatives to consider Western draft of projected joint statement. All four (United Kingdom, France, Canada, Italy) approved without too much difficulty, and draft was delivered to Union of Soviet Socialist Republics as acceptable to us.

4:00 P.M. Back to Committee 1, where no unusual developments were visible. East European supporters of Union of Soviet Socialist Republics having usual monolithic field day —almost identical speeches to a depleted audience.

5:00 P.M. Consultation at the request of the Representative of Pakistan. He had heard rumors about a big Soviet "ploy," did not know what it was, but mistrusted the whole picture. Five other Delegations sent word shortly after 5:00 P.M. that there was something "cooking" but nobody knew what. United States Mission to the United Nations, having notified Washington immediately after lunch, decided to relax rather than "run scared." Session of First Committee ended without any "ploy."

6:00 P.M. With Mrs. Wadsworth to Austrian reception at United Nations Members' Dining Room. Austrian Representative unusually warm in comment on disarmament situation. Had apparently been told about projected joint statement, heartily approved, as did most Delegates, who miraculously find these things out. However, since neither we nor the Soviet Union was particularly interested in secrecy at this point, Soviet Representative and I agreed that we would not attempt denial, merely adopt "wait and see."

6:45 P.M. Also with Mrs. Wadsworth, to reception of Argentina at the St. Regis. Similar stories, similar reactions, no new rumors, question of big Soviet "ploy" discounted as having been artificially raised as possible smoke screen (for what?).

8:00 P.M. Dinner given by Canadian Delegation in honor of Foreign Minister and Members of Parliament returning to Ottawa. Wives invited. Considerable frank conversation and criticism of each other's views; some speculation as to the stability of the present government, but eventual mutual expression of concern and esteem. These people are sometimes more American than we are!

11:30 P.M. Bed.

Wednesday, 9:00 A.M. Top staff meeting. Received reports that great satisfaction being expressed from all quarters at story of United States–Union of Soviet Socialist Republics cooperation on joint disarmament statement. Discussed possibility of postponing further debate until issuance. Staff chief will contact Committee Chairman.

9:30 A.M. Full Delegation meeting continued discussion on postponing debate. Drafting group reported striking some snags but only on wording—hoped to have a draft by mid-afternoon. Several Delegates question United States position on colonialism. Suggested they draw up changes they would like to see made.

10:30 A.M. Emergency meeting with Chairman of First Committee on possibilities of postponement. Present in addition to United States and Union of Soviet Socialist Republics: United Kingdom, France, Canada, Italy, Bulgaria, Czechoslovakia, Poland, and three Delegates who were listed to speak this morning. Agreed to postpone morning session, take another reading at 2:00 P.M.

11:00 A.M. Long session with United Kingdom, France, Canada, and Italy on tentative joint draft, necessitating conference phone calls with State Department officials. Final agreement unless Union of Soviet Socialist Republics demands further changes. Sketched out possible fall-back position for use only if imperative.

1:00 P.M. Luncheon given by Norwegian Representative, whose Foreign Minister is staying in New York another week. Frank conversation about usefulness of "cooperation" technique, discussion in general terms about contents of joint statement. Indian Representative took pains to warn me that he could not support us on too rigid a position. Reminded him that this was his traditional posture and told him he should sit in Geneva for three months and find out for himself who was the rigid one. "Perhaps I will!" he said darkly. What have I done?

2:30 P.M.   Staff informs me that Union of Soviet Socialist Republics has demanded only insignificant change. Called United Kingdom and indicated willingness to buy for sake of speed and atmosphere. He agreed and will inform the others, while I check with Washington and make arrangements for duplication, translation, and publication as United Nations document, also to postpone afternoon session.

3:30 P.M.   After completing arrangements above, held brief consultation with Union of Soviet Socialist Republics Representative, who professes himself delighted with developments. I suggest, and he agrees, that we will try to refrain from further debate ourselves and use our good offices to persuade others to keep it short and sweet. Discussed very briefly possibility of jointly sponsored resolution—will have real talk on this later.

4:00 P.M.   Meet with group from Geneseo, New York, High School (home town) making special trip to visit United Nations.

4:30 P.M.   Meet with Indian Representative to discuss joint statement and plans for further debate. He reports Afro-Asian group much encouraged by signs of cooperation. I warned of overoptimism. He asked about resolution, saying that he had in mind one which could be accepted by both sides, which is difficult, if not impossible. Left whole matter in abeyance since joint statement will not be distributed until morning.

5:00 P.M.   Brief meeting with Secretary General and Under Secretaries Andrew Cordier and Ralph Bunche on matters having to do with the Headquarters Agreement. Cautious optimism that we can complete Assembly session on time and without undue explosions. Told them of past two days' activities on disarmament item, which of course they knew all about. Got from them that reports received of favorable reaction were not exaggerated. I warned against overoptimism, which makes people feel that much worse if things go wrong.

6:00 P.M.   With Mrs. Wadsworth to reception by New

Zealand Representative, whose Foreign Minister did not come this year. Held in United Nations Members' Dining Room— very convenient for working staffs, also has invaluable asset for a diplomatic reception: an escape hatch, or alternate exit. Ballroom of the Plaza only other place in town in general use with such facility.

6:50 P.M.   Reception by Representative of the Philippines at (of all places!) the Plaza. Here found much buzzing among Afro-Asian members, but could not ferret out the reason. Probably find out in the morning. Again had to warn of over-enthusiasm in several quarters, but this seems to be an example of how members really feel about the Cold War and mindless friction. Will write special report to Washington on this if all goes well next few days.

8:00 P.M.   Small dinner given by Chinese Ambassador at very nice Chinese restaurant. Minimum of shop talk, maximum of relaxation, at least twenty different courses for dinner. This job is murder on the waistline!

11:00 P.M.   Home and bed comparatively early in spite of all the courses!

Thursday, 9:00 A.M.   Top staff meeting reveals that buzzing among Afro-Asian group last night was due to sudden meeting called by Indian Representative to discuss disarmament situation. Not clear what he wanted except to draft resolution, represent full Afro-Asian group in negotiations on it, etc. Expect more information later.

10:30 A.M.   Committee 1 launching of joint statement with brief remarks by United States and Union of Soviet Socialist Republics. A few questions, all introduced with laudatory remarks. Photographers and newsmen swarming; agreed to set up press conference for noon.

11:15 A.M.   Met with group representing the Citizens Foundation of Syracuse, New York. Gave short briefing and answered questions; met a few old friends from political days.

12:00 NOON. Press conference. Hasty consultation with
Soviets brought agreement that we should meet the press
separately, lest an attempt be made to play us off against each
other like a ping-pong match. I won the toss and took first
crack. Questions nearly all confined to the joint document,
seeking clarification of various points. Turned aside long-
distance questions as to creation of new atmosphere, etc., em-
phasized considerable areas of disagreement still preventing
treaty, etc. Heard later that Soviet had taken almost exactly
same line; only a few standard uncomplimentary remarks
about imperialist, warmongering United States.

1:15 P.M. Annual luncheon of the Foreign Policy Association downtown. Medium-length ad-lib speech about how
things were going—perhaps half an hour of questions. Very
friendly and relaxing but wish didn't have to talk shop *all* the
time.

3:00 P.M. Committee 1 resumes debate, with several Latin
Americans and Afro-Asians on the list. Tried to listen to all,
but kept getting called to phone (Washington) and other
consultations. Soviet Representative, in very brief chat, said
he had come to the conclusion that trying to work out a
jointly sponsored resolution with me would put too much
responsibility and strain on us and on the temporarily happy
atmosphere. I agreed, having received instructions to soft-
pedal idea. Possibly best deal would be nonaligned group
working with both of us. Will talk more later. Talks with
Austrians, Swedes, Indians, Burmese, and others revealed
dozens of different possibilities. Told them all: Make it short,
make it anodyne, do not express partiality for either side if
you want a big vote. Otherwise, of course, we would like
their help!

5:00 P.M. Representative of Ireland wanted to know if
any Washington reaction to his resolution to keep ownership
or custody of atomic weapons from spreading beyond where
they are now. Told him United States could not support be-

cause of long-range plans, hoped he would not feel he had to push it.

6:00 P.M. With Mrs. Wadsworth to Representative of Burma's reception, United Nations Members' Dining Room. Everyone buzzing about resolutions on disarmament. At least six separate ones in view, including one being peddled by India. We have not seen it but are told it has tentative Soviet approval.

6:30 P.M. Also with Mrs. Wadsworth to reception of Representative of Ethiopia. Even more buzzing. Was told flatly that many Africans and Asians not anxious to follow Indian leadership. They suspect too close a tie with Soviets, although latter have now announced Indian resolution unacceptable. The wires are hot to Washington tonight.

7:00 P.M. Still with Mrs. Wadsworth, reception of Representative of Ceylon at the Plaza. Buzzing finally subsiding, calm returning. Soviet Delegates most affable. Beware.

8:00 P.M. Dinner with Representative of France at his residence. Stag. Nothing but shop. Secretary General, two of his top men do their best to lighten atmosphere. French show considerable disgust with wild rumor factory, readiness of Delegates to believe that everything is sweetness and light when no basic attitudes have changed. Some profess dislike for resolution so meaningless as to command heavy if not unanimous vote; would raise hopes too high. I remind again that strong resolution would be useless even if it endorses our position. Not only will Soviet bloc vote against and refuse to heed it in negotiations, but large number of nonaligned must abstain. Better, we think, to pass anodyne resolution and warn continuously against overoptimism.

12:15 A.M. Bed, too late.

Friday, 9:00 A.M. Top staff meeting; all events and results of week rehashed; all new telegrams and instruction telegrams checked.

9:30 A.M.   Truncated Delegation meeting—heavy absenteeism. Forecast schedule for next week. Draft presented on United States position in regard colonialism: generally well received but considered impossible to act on without full Delegation since it requests Department to change certain elements of the official position paper. Postponed.

10:00 A.M.   Group of Delegations with offices in the Empire State Building call to protest certain new parking regulations. Deputation of three ride to La Guardia Airport, agree to meeting with Police and Traffic Commissioners early next week.

10:30 A.M.   Leave La Guardia for Washington.

11:40 A.M.   Arrive Washington.

12:00 NOON.   Cabinet meeting at White House. Short and businesslike. Secretary of State spoke briefly about United Nations General Assembly. I spoke even more briefly. President and two others asked questions.

1:00 P.M.   Lunch with Secretary of State and top staff. Rehashed all activities thoroughly, received general approval; forecast of things to come, and tentative agreement on how we will handle them. Department ready to consider Delegation's ideas on colonialism but pointed out change would be difficult in midstream unless sudden switch in situation.

2:00 P.M.   House Appropriations Subcommittee holding hearing on State Department request for United States Mission. Most of time spent arguing on need for new building for security reasons. Chairman Rooney wants to know what Committee on Public Works is going to do on major building request. (Chairman Thomas hints approval.)

3:30 P.M.   Fly to New York.

4:40 P.M.   Arrive New York.

5:30 P.M.   Address meeting of group from National Defense College of Canada. Half an hour speaking, fifteen minutes questions. Main interest in disarmament since Canada is member of negotiating group. Found that in common with many other military groups, this one has strong desire for disarmament. Convinced that arms race holds no security; deterrence cannot work for much longer. Most of them rather discouraged; they should be.

6:30 P.M. With Mrs. Wadsworth to reception given by Belgian Representative, whose Foreign Minister went home weeks ago. Received reports on disarmament debate from various sources. Most speeches now dull; lack of forensics ascribed to joint statement. It appears we have damped down the fires considerably. Big argument still raging as to whether partisan or anodyne resolution should be tried, with apparent trend toward latter.

7:00 P.M. Also with Mrs. Wadsworth, to reception given by Japanese Representative, who, I learn, spoke today in very somber tone. As only country against which A-bomb has been used, they command considerable respect and attention. Their line seems to be: very strong appeal against manufacture, testing, and ownership of nuclear weapons, very strong demand on atomic and other great powers to come to terms before it is too late, no indication of favoring proposals of either side. If they should sponsor this sort of thing, it would get a lot of votes, but neither Soviets nor we could support it as of now.

7:30 P.M. Also with Mrs. Wadsworth, to reception by Representative of Poland—no Foreign Minister in evidence. Much talk about Japanese line, but satellites apparently all instructed to play it down as requiring too much too soon. Soviet Ambassador very friendly (always more so, I find, at their own or their allies' parties), says he assumes we can't vote for Japanese idea. I took an "Oh, I don't know" line, which may or may not keep him guessing. Rather doubt it.

Fortunately no dinner scheduled for tonight, so home early and horizontal soonest.

Saturday, 9:00 A.M. Meeting with legal counsel. Reviewed parking situation for Empire State Building tenants, also status of bill introduced in New York State Legislature to extend the exemption from local taxation beyond the radius distance from U.N. Headquarters now allowed. Soviet and Afghan residences now outside the charmed circle, but refuse to pay because they don't tax our diplomats' residences in Russia or Afghanistan.

10:00 A.M. Meeting with Mayor, Police Commissioner, tax experts, and Traffic Commissioner at City Hall. Quick review of situations; decisions: for the Empire State Building's tenants, set aside two or three blocks in mid-thirties between Park and Madison Avenues but hold fast on forbidding them to park on Thirty-fourth Street right at building entrance. For the tax situation, Mayor Wagner will notify Governor of New York that New York City approves bill and urges its passage and signing.

11:30 A.M. Informal press conference upon arrival at United Nations Headquarters. Purely fishing expedition for press, with usual rumors to be confirmed or denied; why have I come to see Hammarskjöld on a Saturday? (It's his favorite day.) Whose resolution on disarmament will pass? Would I comment on Senator Blank's blast at one of the Asian diplomats and the possibilities of an international incident arising from it? (Senator Blank is free and over twenty-one; besides, he is a United States Senator, etc.)

12:00 NOON. Brief meeting with Secretary General to run over latest developments in an alleged espionage case involving an employee of the United Nations Secretariat and an employee of an Iron Curtain Delegation. Agreed that evidence was probably sufficient without adding to it further; action to be taken. Reminded Secretary General of his annual date to have Christmas dinner with the Wadsworths; received reassurance.

1:00 P.M. Luncheon given by Mayor Wagner at the Waldorf to honor a visiting chief of state. Too much lunch, too many speeches, but fortunately not much shop talk.

3:00 P.M.   Quick trip to office to catch up on mail and phone calls.

4:00 P.M.   Relocation (in fact, oblivion, at home).

8:00 P.M.   Formal dinner party at United Kingdom residence in Riverdale, in honor of visiting royalty. (White tie, tails, decorations.) Luckily, little shop talk except that United Kingdom Minister (second in command) told me we were running into difficulties with our program for Arab refugees and might have to review the whole business. Apparently, Saudi Arabia and the United Arab Republic, although not very friendly to each other, were dragging their feet in the Special Political Committee on the text of an already agreed resolution and would have to be "seen" and "talked to." Assigned top deputy to this, as former United States member on Palestine Conciliation Commission. Hoped for the best; waited until ranking guest gave signal, went home.

12:00 MIDNIGHT.   Fell into bed.

Sunday, 11:00 A.M.   (We didn't sleep late—just didn't have to start work as early.) To United Nations Headquarters to participate with Soviet Representative and others on CBS television show, "U.N. in Action." Subject was disarmament, format was individual interviews with Larry Lesueur. No particularly bad moments except possibly when Larry asked Soviet Representative how he thought United States and West were reacting to the latest Soviet proposals (absolutely unacceptable) and the Soviet with gimlet eye and a mirthless smile, said: "Why don't you ask Ambassador Wadsworth that question? There he sits, right over there!" Quick curtain by Lesueur, although this time I might have been willing to have a slugging match, as many times before and since.

1:30 P.M.   With Mrs. Wadsworth to luncheon given by the Representative of Colombia at his residence (rented) out on Long Island. Very quiet, happy, relaxed, no shop talk at all except for amusing anecdotes about mutual friends. The word "rented" in parentheses because he is not interested in local taxation as per yesterday A.M.'s meeting.

4:00 P.M.   Back to the Embassy residence to receive Indian Representative and his chief deputy. Our Indian friend propounded the opinion that the United States was not on the level in the whole disarmament business (no comment); and wound up with a long tirade against Pakistan on the subject of Kashmir.

7:00 P.M.   Buffet supper at United States Embassy—mixed bag, including diplomats, relatives, business friends, and just friends. Everyone too tired to think, or "too pooped to pop," so evening was smashing success. A touch of music, informal songs, and recitations, and a general spirit of camaraderie.

11:00 P.M.   Bed!

As any reader can tell, very few matters came to a head during the week, at least to the point where they could be bragged about. Certain reasonable things were done and said. That is the way the world goes, and that is the way the United Nations goes. On looking back, I feel I have not made one outstanding fact clear: Namely, that at all the receptions and dinners, and even a goodly number of the luncheons, my wife, as an indispensable member of the team, was there and active. This is very important for evaluation.

Not only was she present, but she made her presence known as a member of the team from the very first day. She managed to get along with people whose national positions made such a relationship most difficult for me; she got along famously with our friends, forthrightly with our antagonists, and outstandingly with the nonaligned people. I doubt very much whether I or the victim will ever forget the afternoon when she approached the Indian Representative with measured tread and level eye at a reception given by the United States in the Empire Room of the Waldorf and asked: "Tell me, Krishna, why do you insist on carrying that cane around with you all the time? You know perfectly well you are not lame; whom are you trying to fool?"

Whereupon Krishna Menon, with a flash of his black eyes and a wave of the cane, responded: "But, of course, my dear lady! I am not lame and have never pretended to be. This is merely part of my costume, just as some people will wear spats, and others will sport a monocle. I seem to remember several Americans and British who practiced such small oddities, and it happens to suit my purpose to carry a cane."

The upshot of this was that Menon promised Mrs. Wadsworth one of his old canes "when he was through with it," and always from then on held her in solid esteem. You will have to ask my wife whether she ever received a cane, but to this day, the devastating frankness of her approach won her a place in his difficult heart that precious few Americans can claim.

Another of the prickly pears Mrs. Wadsworth and I frequently encountered was Andrei Y. Vishinsky, Chief of the Union of Soviet Socialist Republics Delegation until his death in 1954. He was a brilliant, sarcastic, ruthless man, responsible for the snuffing out of no one knows how many lives in the various purges in Russia as well as in some of the satellite states. At the same time, he was a man of humor, with a deep love of family and a great appreciation of music, who might occasionally be found at an informal party singing Russian, Polish or French songs with great enjoyment.

My most memorable meeting with him occurred toward the close of one of the innumerable receptions it was part of my job to attend. Leaving the party, Mrs. Wadsworth and I entered a half-filled elevator. More and more people crowded in, pushing us backward, ever backward. Finally the door slid shut, and I heard a strangled yelp behind me calling out in French: *"Au secours! au secours! Je suis accablé par un éléphant!"* ("Help! help! I'm being overwhelmed by an elephant!") Craning my neck hard, I found little Vishinsky (about five feet two inches) crushed between me and the wall, grinning wickedly as he cried out. Ever after, he called me *"Monsieur l'Éléphant"* to my face, although one of his staff told me after his death that among the Soviet delegation he used to refer to me as *"Monsieur l'Éléphant avec le Coeur."*

An animal story of a slightly different quality occurred outside the U.N. proper and involved Anthony Nutting, one of the United Kingdom's seemingly inexhaustible store of top-flight professional diplomats, as well as men from political life who manage to adopt the professional outlook when placed in the comparatively strange environs of diplomacy. Among the U.K. diplomats I have served with—Sir Gladwyn Jebb, Sir Pierson Dixon, and Sir Patrick, and many others— Tony Nutting ranks as one of the most able and delightful of all. He also had a pixie sense of humor second to none, a trait that popped out in the most unexpected places, and Mrs. Wadsworth and I were saddened when he broke off a brilliant career in mid-flight and resigned from the government over the Suez Canal incident of 1956.

Our story begins at the end of the sessions of the Subcommittee of the Disarmament Commission, in May of 1955, when Mrs. Wadsworth presented him with a small mouse carved out of wood. He immediately named it Louise. Some months later, he was a participant in a most serious television show that featured highly placed personalities from different parts of the world, each interviewed at his own desk. The correspondent who interviewed Mr. Nutting, then United Kingdom Minister of State for Foreign Affairs, noted that his desk was unusually uncluttered and neat for a man of his many interests, and remarked upon it, adding: "Don't you even have pictures of your family on your desk, Mr. Minister?"

"Why no," said Tony, "I don't. Except for Louise, of course. This is Louise"—he held the tiny mouse up to the camera—"and she was given to me by the wife of my American colleague, Ambassador Wadsworth." The interviewer moved hastily to the more serious subjects of the day.

So passes a truly typical week at the Glass House when it is working full time. There are no exaggerations in it, and I imagine that either Ambassador Lodge or Ambassador Goldberg might consider it enviably restful and quiet. I hope, perhaps, that it will give you some sort of understanding as to what your Representatives in the United Nations are up against from day to day. I have purposely left out the ghastly stories of the shoe-pounding week of 1960, with Castro and his chicken-feathered crew bounding from hotel to hotel. I have left out incipient crises with African diplomats who were convinced they were being discriminated against for any number of reasons, cases where Delegates had killed United States citizens in traffic accidents, where foreign Delegations' employees had been mugged in Central Park, or where other Delegations' employees had been picked up for improperly soliciting policemen in the park. All these other things happened, and happened only too often, but the day-to-day routine didn't need these pieces of icing on the cake to make them notable.

10 · Potentials

The Glass House observed its twentieth birthday in June, 1965, and from present indications it looks as though this emergence from the teens will be accompanied by even louder and more menacing rumbles than in the past. I rather doubt that anyone can produce a crystal ball of such clarity and power that the future can be predicted with confidence, but it should not be impossible to indulge in speculation based on observation of the past and present. Such speculation could take into consideration the recognizable and predictable patterns of reaction among the various tenants of the Glass House, but must, I fear, be based upon certain assumptions.

The first assumption is that a large percentage of the peoples and governments of the world will continue to believe in the necessity for an active and trustworthy voluntary association to which they can belong and to which they can entrust certain types of problems that are not readily solved by bilateral diplomacy or by regional organization efforts. Anyone who expects or demands more than that from the United Nations in the immediate future simply has not learned from the past and present. In order to survive with respect and dignity, the House must keep a cold and realistic eye upon its limitations and must not bite off more than it can chew. Neither should it attempt a self-strengthening campaign until virtually the whole membership is ready for it and willing to support it.

Let us never forget that earlier associations, notably the League of Nations, failed not only because of structural or policy weakness in themselves, but because the members were not ready to live up to their obligations. If we were able, by majority vote, to put certain teeth in appropriate places in the Charter—a miracle so remote as to be out of sight today—we would still have to worry about whether the minority would obey the mandates of the United Nations or accept punishment of some sort for defying them. I clearly recall the 1954 debate in the General Assembly over the question of holding a conference on revision of the Charter in 1955. By a rare twist of irony, it was the Representative of the Soviet Union who best expressed the majority opinion at that time. There is no need to revise the Charter in any way, he explained; all that is needed is for each member to live up to the provisions it now contains! Ergo, change in the Charter is also remote.

In thus relating the strength of the organization directly to the steadfast support of its members, we are also recognizing another fact that is usually lost in the welter of confusion about the Glass House. This is that the United Nations, as successor to the League of Nations, is not and is not meant to be the last step in man's journey from the cave to the ideal state. Since the journey is purely evolutionary, and since the ideal is still far short of attainment, we must look on the Glass House as simply another step, and the best one yet, in that process. I have heard strong opponents of world government agree with and applaud that theory, and it may perhaps put in better perspective the position of the Glass House in contemporary history as well as the past. No one knows, of course, what the "ideal" is, so that no one can measure just how far we have progressed along the road and how much further we may have to go. Perhaps there is no well-defined end that people will recognize, and that would be just as well, lest everyone relax his efforts for improvement at exactly the wrong moment.

The second assumption we must make is that the Glass House will have been able to survive the storms of the Nineteenth General Assembly without too much damage to its structure. This is a different and comparatively pinpointed assumption compared to the first, since it dares to predict that the quarrel over nonpayment of Soviet, French, and other dues can be satisfactorily solved. It is difficult to envision a satisfactory solution unless those in arrears pay up somehow, and the method is not as important as the payment. Anything less would be surrender of a most vital principle, and a setting of precedent that could destroy the organization in any case. Therefore, to those who argue that adherence to principle might cause a walkout and a serious weakening, if not collapse, of the structure, I answer that to allow the arrears to go completely unchallenged would surely (note that I do not say "might") cause such a collapse, since the General Assembly, by failing to find an answer, would clear the way for general defiance, which would result in bankruptcy.

The storms of the Nineteenth General Assembly, however, will probably not exceed in violence many other disturbances that from time to time have battered at the foundations of the Glass House. They seem huge and terrifying when seen close up, but so did several others that were safely survived by the organization. One thing that tends to frighten many observers is the habit that Soviet Representatives so often indulge in: the use of the word "never." I cannot count the number of times I have heard: "The Union of Soviet Socialist Republics will never agree!" to a certain policy or course of action. Former Premier Khrushchev, Foreign Minister Gromyko, Deputy Foreign Ministers Kuznetsov and Zorin, Ambassadors Vishinsky, Malik, Zaroubin, Sobolev, Tsarapkin—all of them and more, at various times but with utmost fervor, have proclaimed undying opposition, only to adopt the same policy or course of action as their own in the long run.

And so crisis after crisis has passed, sometimes because of flexibility on the part of the "opposition," sometimes because of the realization on our part that we could and should improve our position. By and large, however, there has been no unconditional and abject surrender on either side. On both sides, it has often been advantageous to demonstrate a certain amount of flexibility, although never enough to destroy the particular position. The same thing applies to the willingness to remain at the table during international conferences—regardless of the rightness or wrongness of one's position, it is axiomatic in a "peace-loving" member that he repeatedly state his willingness to negotiate even though he may be determined "never" to give in.

Looking toward the future, then, on the basis of the two assumptions of general desire for an organization like the Glass House and the specific survival of that structure, we may anticipate several minor and a few major developments in the years immediately ahead. On the basis of the realization that the House has a comparatively clear and level future, we should expect virtually all indebtedness to be cleaned up. The very few that may remain in the financial doghouse could doubtless make arrangements of one kind or another to advance enough on account to qualify under Article 19.

Next, we can anticipate that the members most vitally interested in the Glass House will reinforce their support in all kinds of ways. These members are, generally speaking, the newly emergent nations, who need the sponsorship and aid of the United Nations and its Specialized Agencies in order to become more viable economically and therefore politically. These new states of Africa and Asia, therefore, far from being the menace that some feared, will become the most benignly powerful bloc of the United Nations, not because of geographic or political organization, but because they want and need the United Nations so much that they can bring great pressure to bear against members inclined to fish in roiled waters and generally to keep things off balance.

Their thrust in this regard will be totally nonaligned. Most of them have had personal experience in the tactics of the power blocs and want no part of being caught in the middle, and even less of being captive to either side. Rather than sit helplessly by while the major protagonists wrangle endlessly, these members can be counted on to help bring the parties to a quarrel back to rational discussion, to ward off possible harm to the international family of nations. At the same time, of course, they will continue to press for such schemes as will bring them quickly out of the fiscal quicksands that they have found so prevalent. Some of these schemes the more wealthy members not only can afford but should and will embrace; others are unsound and self-defeating.

Next, I think that the United Nations will become increasingly impatient with the tragic, vicious bilateral quarrels based on hatred and little else. One would, of course, be stupid not to credit the feelings of those who believe themselves the victims of deliberate campaigns, both military and propagandistic. At the same time, I believe that the next decade will see the gradual development of a conviction in international circles that mankind cannot afford to allow these quarrels to muddy the waters of cooperation. While sympathizing up to a point with those who claim to be victims of aggression, we will see a strong trend toward "a plague on both your houses" and firm measures to deny these people the luxury of private quarrels. With the world as it is today, a private quarrel simply cannot remain private; if there is no appropriate treaty provision, there is always the lighthearted and thoughtless promise to help out in a "war of liberation." See Cyprus!

Something else that now seems to be unstoppable is the eventual universality of the Glass House. Wholly apart from the extremely emotional subject of mainland China, and also apart from the sometimes doubtful rush to enroll the shiny new states emerging from colonial status into independence, formulas will doubtless be found to bring the divided states of Germany, Korea, and Vietnam into the picture. The potential of the membership here, particularly in Germany, is too powerful and important to remain for long outside the gates.

Little by little, as these political trends make themselves felt, the realization will grow that war is useless as a tool of national policy. Added to the lip service that is being given this subject today will come the determination not to jeopardize the future of one's country and mankind itself by insisting on ever-increasing armaments. The exact point at which all the important world leaders will be willing (and free) to back up their public statements on the futility of war with meaningful negotiations is not known or even guessed at. But it will come because it must come. Otherwise, man has no future. And the Glass House, whose record on disarmament is one of unrelieved failure, will be a tool and a beneficiary as well. And because the Glass House will then finally be speaking for mankind, the human race, scarcely deserving of such good fortune today, will be the final beneficiary.

While all these things are happening on the political front, equally great strides will be made on the economic and social fronts. The invaluable work done by the agencies described in Chapters 2 and 3 of this book will be doubled and redoubled. Gradually the heavy burden assumed unilaterally by the United States and a few others will be dispersed throughout the House and its agencies, where we will get far more for our foreign-aid dollar than we do now. By utilizing the savings realized from whatever disarmament agreements can be made from time to time for the welfare of people rather than for their destruction, resources scarcely dreamed of before will be available.

How long will all this take? What assurance have we that any of it will happen? What are we going to do about Communism? How are we going to keep the United Nations on the right track? The answers to these and many other questions are simply not at hand. I don't know; you don't know, none of the governments or their top officials know. But I have faith that if my two basic assumptions are anywhere near valid, the rest is bound to follow. The good things that can happen, can happen only if there is a Glass House in existence and in working order. Without it, a few good things could happen, but we would all be scrambling to build another Glass House lest the inhabitants of a Pandora's box be allowed to take over civilization. Then we would be fortunate indeed if we could build a new one in time!

If I were a pessimist, I might be shouting "Wake up, America!" and various other alarms. There is no question that some Americans should wake up, and with a few it is absolutely imperative in order to save our skins, but that is not the way things get done. The way something gets done is by convincing the people that it is the right, it is the necessary, it is the sensible thing to do. You don't frighten people into supporting the United Nations, any more than you have frightened them into building a nationwide bomb-shelter system. All the things we read about nuclear weapons, about how many other countries will probably have the bomb within a few years—these apparently don't convince people that they should learn to get along with their neighbors, internationally speaking.

What I am trying to say is that we have a great tool if we want to use it. It has done us far more good than it has any other great power; it has monotonously done our bidding, sometimes even at the expense of our friends. It has helped us to overwhelm our enemies with votes and to hold potential troublemakers in abeyance. Now that it has demonstrated for two decades that it makes sense for us and our friends, what more logical use could be made of it than to demonstrate its true usefulness for all of mankind? If we recognize the world as it is rather than as we would have it, then we have a chance of survival. But to survive, one needs a bulwark. As the United Nations Association has so well put it: "Where would we be without the United Nations?"

Yet the same barrier I have mentioned repeatedly, that of sovereignty or selfishness, keeps every member of the Glass House from being a truly full-fledged member of an international family. And as long as that barrier exists, this organization of ours has a murky future. Perhaps we should look backward for a moment and see if we cannot regain some of that perspective I talk about so much. We find, of course, that military alliances have existed since the very dawn of history, both offensive and defensive. Primitive man clustered together for safety from human or animal enemies, but his coming together was rarely if ever for any other reason.

Little by little, the idea of alliance for strength and resultant safety began to develop into faint stirrings of alliance for economic viability and social togetherness. Guilds, associations like the Hanseatic League, societies, religions, Knights Templar and of Malta, Freemasonry—all these and many more came almost imperceptibly to the fore and established themselves in the societies emerging from the old civilization. The Renaissance period, the Industrial Revolution, the image of the indentured servant changing into the self-respecting wage earner—all these played their part. Finally the governments, starting with the Magna Carta, yielded bit by bit to the governed and their rights, listened to the voice and mind of the people themselves.

How can we complain over the barriers and the slow path of evolution when we see how far mankind has come? Even twenty years ago you couldn't have found a corporal's guard predicting that an international organization representing 117 sovereign governments would be flourishing today, and that another few years might see the entire roster of earthly governments in the fold. People change very gradually, but institutions change in leaps and bounds at times. And no matter where you go in the world these days, you will find man clustering in dozens of different ways: sometimes from sheer gregariousness, but more often because he has found it to be in his interest to cluster.

Churches, civic clubs, social clubs, labor unions, veterans' organizations, political parties, learned societies, chambers of commerce, boards of trade, industrial associations, medical associations, legal associations, bankers associations—invariably they exist for help and advancement of the members in one form or other. People are joiners, and now so are their governments. From town meetings to municipal associations, from mayors' groups and governors' councils to federations of states and republics scattered all over the world. And on a grander scale there are NATO, CENTO, and SEATO, the Organization of American States, the Warsaw Pact and the Arab League, and the British Commonwealth and any number of alliances, treaties, pacts, and agreements on a bilateral basis.

Tiring just to think about, isn't it—all this joining? Yet the question arises inexorably: If there is so much desire for joining both on the part of people and their governments, why can't they do a better job of togetherness in the Glass House? Whence and why and whither the sovereign selfishness? Answer: Evolution is rarely the hare; more often the tortoise. Man clusters socially because that has been acceptable and has proved profitable for many thousands of years. Man clusters economically because that has proved profitable for more than a thousand years. Man clusters politically because that has proved in his interest for many centuries.

But government clustering, outside of purely military agreements, is much more recent, and only since the turn of the twentieth century has international clustering become really respectable. Governments as well as people have to learn what is profitable by experience, not by theory. This takes time, yet we are often so impatient that we begrudge a few decades to the tortoise of evolution. Experience has taught many men that war is outmoded as an instrument of national policy. Most governments have not come to this point as yet because of fear for their own safety. But they will turn around someday and find that old tortoise shuffling up to them.

So with the Glass House and its members—its fans and its detractors. It came to us via the tortoise and will disappear the same way, when another and better concept takes its place. For now, the House is all we have, and if it is sometimes found wanting, it is because of lack of member support rather than intrinsic weakness. I have spent a great deal of space in preceding chapters arguing the value of the United Nations to peoples and to governments, and I will not labor the point here. In my own private crystal ball, however, I see difficult but eventually successful years ahead, with a gradual abatement of Cold War wrangling and jangling, a gradual acceptance of the values involved for the price charged, and finally, a metamorphosis into the kind of world rule through world law that will arrive, via tortoise, only when mankind is ready for it.